The Flea Markets of France

❖

THE
Flea Markets
of
FRANCE

by

SANDY PRICE

photographs by

EMILY LAXER

THE LITTLE BOOKROOM
New York

©2009 The Little Bookroom
©2009 Sandy Price
Photographs ©2009 Emily Laxer

Cover design: Pia Jane Bijkerk
Book design: Laura Jane Coats – Sous le Parapluie
Book production: Adam Hess

Library of Congress Cataloging-in-Publication Data

Price, Sandy.
The flea markets of France / by Sandy Price ; photographs by Emily Laxer.
p. cm.
A follow-up to her Exploring the flea markets of France. 1999.
Includes bibliographical references.
ISBN 1-892145-59-6 (alk. paper)
1. Flea markets--France—Handbooks, manuals, etc. I. Title.
HF5482.15.P743 2008
381'.1920944—dc22
                                        2008030421
Published by The Little Bookroom
435 Hudson St., 3rd floor
New York, NY 10014
www.littlebookroom.com
editorial@littlebookroom.com

10 9 8 7 6 5 4 3 2

Printed in China

*Note: Flea Markets that are described in detail are listed in upper case;
those mentioned in brief are in upper and lower case.*

The Flea Market Experience

FLEA MARKETS OFFER VISITORS A UNIQUE INSIGHT INTO THE FRENCH *ART DE VIVRE*. THE OBJECTS FOR SALE PROVIDE A GLIMPSE OF EVERYDAY LIFE IN decades past, and also suggest how that heritage continues to resonate today. As well, the markets illustrate the huge regional diversity of France—in culture, lifestyle, economic activity and design.

Beyond all of this, the markets offer visitors something normally very difficult to achieve—a foray into French society today. Strolling along taking in the scene, you are participating with the French in one of their favorite pastimes—*la chine*, which in English roughly means "searching for finds."

Visiting the French flea markets is a surprisingly easy thing for travelers to do. The markets are very accessible and fit readily into your sightseeing plans. Most are held in the center of town, and are simple to get to on foot or by public transport. You choose the time you want to go and how long you want to stay. No admission fee is charged and there is no guide telling you what to observe. But while easy, there are a few tips that will help you negotiate the markets and enhance your experience.

WHEN TO GO

The number of vendors and the liveliness of the flea markets can vary, depending on the season. Not surprisingly, during the winter, particularly in the north, the markets tend to be smaller and quieter than at other times of the year. (If you are looking for bargains, though, this may be when you will make your best finds.) In the summer, on the other hand, it can be hot and the markets crowded, especially in the south. The French generally take their holidays in August, joining all the other summer visitors at the popular tourist destinations. On balance, the early fall and late spring are perhaps the best times to come, but check seasonal weather patterns for the area you are going to visit, before you make your plans.

If you are a collector or serious bargain hunter, try to get to the markets early in the day, as that is when your chances of a great find are best. Otherwise, I suggest arriving mid-morning, when the markets are more lively and animated. At midday, the crowds thin out and vendors sit down alongside their booths for the serious business of eating lunch (which can be an elaborate affair, often including a bottle of wine). While they are still available to negotiate with you, this is not the best time to try to engage their attention. After lunch, even though the market is listed as all-day, vendors may start to pack up mid-afternoon, so if you want to be sure to catch the action, come earlier.

HOW TO GET THERE

Whether you should travel by car or train depends on where you plan to go. If you anticipate visiting many smaller communities within a large region, a car is very convenient, both for general sightseeing and visiting the flea markets. However, rentals can be expensive (particularly if you want an automatic), gas is costly (about twice as much as in North America, for example, though mileage is usually much better), and the autoroutes charge hefty tolls. Also, driving in France can be very stressful (the speed limit on the highways is 130 kilometers per hour, but many drive faster than that).

If you mostly plan to visit cities and large towns, seriously consider taking the train. France has a wonderful high-speed rail system, called the TGV (*"trains à grande vitesse"*). Not only very fast and comfortable, the TGV trains are remarkably punctual as well. Be advised, though, that routes tend to be oriented toward Paris (and other major centers). Regional and local trains provide very comprehensive service, but can be a bit less reliable.

If you plan to spend several days traveling by train, consider buying a French rail pass before you leave (available to non-Europeans, these passes must be purchased outside France), which allows you unlimited travel each day. The price is based on the number of days you use the train (beyond a minimum), so you should try to map out your schedule ahead of time. If your objective is to see a lot of flea markets within a few hundred kilometers of Paris, consider basing yourself there, and traveling out to the markets in the morning, returning in the evening. This is a surprisingly easy and convenient way to travel, even large distances. For example, you can get to Strasbourg in less than two and a half hours, even though it is almost 500 kilometers away.

Within cities and towns you can usually access the flea markets by *métro*, bus or tram. (Several French cities boast a very efficient and modern tramway system.) Train stations often have tourist offices where you can get information on how to reach your destination. Not only will public transit save you money, it can also save you time. Driving in French cities is often stressful and confusing, parking hard to come by, and taxis slow and costly.

WHAT TO BRING

Carry as little as possible with you when you go to the markets (though a light

cloth bag for your purchases comes in handy, as vendors often hand out very flimsy ones). Heavy bags and big cameras not only impede easy access to the wares, they quickly label you as a tourist, which may affect the prices you are quoted and your ability to bargain. More important, carrying these items makes you a potential target of pickpockets, sadly all too prevalent in France. If possible, leave your purse at the hotel and carry only a small amount of cash well hidden on your person. And, as for your camera, be advised that many vendors do not like photos being taken. They may well chastise you if you do not obtain permission beforehand, even if only taking a picture of their wares.

If you are traveling by car, and visiting the markets en route, do not leave your suitcases or other valuables unattended, even if well hidden in the trunk. It is just too risky, as I have learned the hard way. (We once had all our bags stolen from the trunk of our rental car, midday on a busy street in Aix-en-Provence.) Breaking into cars and stealing their contents is a common occurrence in France, as any police officer will tell you.

HOW TO COMMUNICATE

Cultural misunderstandings can occasionally arise in everyday dealings between the French- and the English-speaking worlds, causing confusion and resentment on both sides. The French tend to observe social formalities that many North Americans, in particular, have abandoned in favor of a more casual approach. Some label the North American style more open, while others consider it too forward, less polite. Conversely, when it comes to the French, what some visitors see as unwelcoming others interpret as simply more reserved.

The best way to negotiate these cultural minefields, in the flea markets and elsewhere, is to recognize that formal expressions of politeness and respect will invariably succeed. Using titles like *monsieur* and *madame* is common here (and often expected), as is saying *bonjour* and *au revoir* with each encounter. Indeed, in smaller communities, customers typically offer a general greeting ("*bonjour, messieurs dames*") as they enter a store, and bid everyone farewell ("*au revoir, messieurs dames*") when leaving.

Another important tip is to try to address people in French—at least initially—even if your command of the language is very limited. It is seen as a form of respect, and a recognition that you are in a foreign country. Try to master a few words (numbers are especially useful in the markets, as elsewhere) and simple expressions. If even a few phrases are beyond you, at least learn to say that you don't speak French and wonder if the other person speaks English. ("*Excusez-moi, madame/monsieur, je ne parle pas français. Est-ce que vous parlez anglais?*") Even though your linguistic difficulties may be painfully obvious, it is polite to acknowledge it. Many vendors (especially in the large tourist centers) speak some English, but they will appreciate any efforts you make to speak their language. Indeed, a few may well resent it if you fail to do so. Don't worry about the quality of your French. It is far more important to show your sensitivity to the culture you are in than to be grammatically correct.

Below are some useful phrases for communicating in the flea markets:

"*S'il vous plaît, monsieur (madame). Ça vaut combien?*"	"Excuse me, sir (madam). How much is this?"
"*La pièce, ou pour l'ensemble?*"	"For one, or all of them?"

"Pourriez-vous m'expliquer...d'où ça vient?"	"Could you tell me...where that comes from?"
"...à quoi ça sert?"	"...what it's for?"
"...comment ça fonctionne?"	"...how it works?"
"C'est joli, mais c'est un peu trop cher pour moi."	"It's nice, but a bit too expensive for me."
"Est-ce votre dernier prix?"	"Is it your lowest price?"
"Pourriez-vous me faire un prix?"	"Could you give me a better price?"
"Est-ce que vous accepteriez...euros?"	"Would you take...euros?"
"Je regrette mais je n'ai pas de monnaie."	"I'm sorry but I don't have the change."
"Merci, je vais y réfléchir."	"Thanks, I'm going to think about it."
"Pourriez-vous l'emballer avec du papier?"	"Could you wrap it in paper?"
"Auriez-vous un sac?"	"Would you have a bag?"

There are a few other words that are useful to know concerning the markets. For example, the term *marché aux puces* often simply refers to flea markets generally. However, *puces* is also used to describe more down-home market wares, while the word *brocante* encompasses mid-range items, equivalent to collectibles. (*Antiquités*, on the other hand, identifies old collectibles, equivalent to antiques in English, narrowly defined.)

Part of the fun of the flea markets, as seasoned veterans readily admit, is feeling that you have made a great find at a good price. Bargaining is an integral component of the market experience in France, so do not be afraid to ask for a price lower than the one quoted. Generally, a ten to 15% reduction will be agreed to without too much difficulty, and even better discounts are possible if the vendor is keen to sell and you are persistent. But the process can be delicate, and requires a combination of tact and finesse.

First, you should have some idea about what the item generally sells for, although this will vary greatly depending on age and condition. Regarding condition, check the prospective purchase over carefully for any defects. Even if you are prepared to buy it with its flaws, they do lower the value and you should at least know what they are. Also, discreetly pointing out defects may help your bargaining efforts. If you push this too far, however, the vendor may become annoyed, and counter that, naturally, any defects were taken into account in setting the price in the first place.

There is a fair amount of theatrics involved in the bargaining process, on the part of buyers and sellers alike. As the purchaser, not appearing wildly keen about the object (that you really covet) is a good idea. Picking it up several times, looking excited and talking to your friend about how nice it is will not help your bargaining position. On the other hand, seeming too indifferent (especially unconvincingly so) may annoy the vendor and get his or her back up. One strategy is to pick up a few things and ask their price before zeroing in on the one you really want. Another idea is to combine something you find really special with another object you are not really interested in, asking the price for both, and then for just the one.

When you have been quoted a figure, it is best to have an idea in your mind of what you are actually willing to pay. Offering an amount that is substantially less than the vendor's quote may cause offense, and lead to your being dismissed as a serious customer. In this regard, an offer significantly less than two-thirds of the asking price is not likely to succeed. You may even find yourself in the embarrassing situation of being denounced in loud tones to others nearby. (Though that may just be part of the vendor's own bargaining strategy, it can be unpleasant.) On the other hand, if you really do find the price much too high, starting to walk away can pan out for you. The vendor may call you back and agree (with dramatic gestures of capitulation, of course) to a reasonable amount.

CHECKING MARKET SCHEDULES

Almost all of the flea markets featured in this book are well-established, having been in existence for many years, if not decades. However, some of those referred to in the section Other Nearby Markets—usually smaller markets—may be more subject to variation. Therefore, before going out of your way, check ahead to verify that they are open. One way is via the internet—a good website for this is www.info-brocantes.com. If you do not have access to the internet, *Antiquités Brocante*, a monthly collectibles magazine, offers a quite reliable list of markets taking place during the month.

A word of caution, though. It is not unusual for markets listed as all-day to begin to wind up in the early afternoon. Your best bet is to arrive in the morning, to avoid any disappointment. Finally, bear in mind that markets listed as on the fourth Saturday or Sunday of the month do not necessarily occur on the last Saturday or Sunday, if there happen to be five weekends that month.

SPECIAL SALES

In addition to the regular markets featured in this book, many communities in France also have special sales, where some wonderful collectibles can be found. If you are in town for a period of time, look for signs advertising a *vide grenier* (emptying the attic), *braderie* (discount sale), or *troc-broc* (brocante exchange). (You are only interested in a *braderie* advertised by an organization, not a store, as the word has a different meaning in the latter case.) These sales may take place in a community hall, church or charity shop. If you don't see anything listed, it is still worth checking at the local tourist office. Also, the magazine *Antiquités Brocante* provides notice of major upcoming events across France. And, if you can, also check the internet sites www.info-brocantes.com and www.vide-greniers.org.

TRANSPORTING YOUR PURCHASES

The best thing to do with your flea market purchases is to bring them home with you in your luggage, if possible. Shipping is a hassle and can add significantly to the cost. If your purchases are breakable, putting them in your carry-on luggage is, of course, preferable. If that is not feasible, wrap them well in your clothing, making sure that they are not in too close contact with each other. Also, a full suitcase packed with lots of clothing offers much better protection for your breakable items than a half-empty one.

21

ABOUT THE REGION

THE VERY NAME "CÔTE D'AZUR" CONJURES UP IMAGES OF A MEDITERRANEAN PARADISE—ROCKY MOUNTAINS MEETING TURQUOISE SEA, AND THE LANDSCAPE in between lush with palms, lemon trees and brilliant flowers. Amazingly, the real thing—despite some overdevelopment here and there—pretty much stands up to the expectation. It is hard to imagine a more stunning coastline than that between Saint-Tropez on the west and Menton, just next to the Italian border, to the east. Yes, it is claustrophobic at times, but it is very hard to beat this region on a sunny winter day, when the wind is calm and you can smell the pines and the eucalyptus trees, and the bougainvillea are blooming in all shades of purple and pink.

The architecture also rises to brilliant heights (some ugly sections notwithstanding). Especially in the east, from Nice to Menton, the towns are awash in all shades of yellow, pink, orange, pale green and blue. A stroll along the seaside is sure to restore anyone's spirits, with the milky, blue-green water meeting brilliant sky on one side, and pastel buildings cascading down to the shore on the other, perhaps edged by a backdrop of rugged cliffs. No wonder that well-heeled British and Russian citizens came here in droves during the dreary winter months in the latter part of the nineteenth and early twentieth centuries.

I have spent several months here over the years, living at the eastern edge of Menton just a few buildings from the Italian border. What a treat it is just to stroll along the winding streets above the sea, lined with nineteenth-century villas, or walk the short distance across the frontier and have a drink at the little pink café dug out of the cliff, overlooking Menton and Cap Martin beyond. (It always amazes me that, within the space of a few hundred meters, suddenly French is replaced by Italian and the quality of the coffee improves.)

The great thing about the Côte d'Azur is that a simple drink, walk or drive here— when it is accompanied by the stunning scenery and lush vegetation of this region —is transformed into something magical. And the best-kept secret is that the experience is available to everyone, regardless of their means. Some may scoff that the Côte d'Azur is reserved for the rich, but it is not true. Sure, the prices of the villas and apartments overlooking the Mediterranean are out of sight. But, even if it does so unwittingly (and against the wishes of some), this region gives everyone who comes here, from nearby or farther afield, the chance to experience the best thing it has to offer—its setting.

ABOUT THE MARKETS

As is often the case in France, the Côte d'Azur flea markets reflect many of the qualities of the region itself. There is a profusion in terms of numbers (if not size), with markets held in just about every community along the coast and also in the more sedate towns of the *arrière pays* above. These are also visually appealing affairs. The settings are often striking; the huge weekly flea market in Nice, for example, takes place in the impossibly lovely and harmonious cours Saleya, in *vieux* Nice, a stone's throw away from the sea.

The markets also reflect the region in terms of the collectibles they offer. The emphasis here is on fine, decorative and ornate objects rather than primitive, functional items (although, interestingly, the more Provençal-looking towns, like Antibes and Valbonne, feature more rustic—albeit very stylish—wares). Here you will find brilliantly colored and elaborately decorated ceramics from Vallauris (near Antibes) and elsewhere in the region, fine silver, crystal, porcelain, paintings, Limoges boxes and sculptures. You will also see high-end men's and women's fashion accessories—jewelry, watches, designer bags, scarves, canes, hats and even fur coats (bizarrely, women often stroll along in fur coats in winter, even though daytime highs rarely dip below 45 to 50 degrees Fahrenheit). Maritime collectibles, not surprisingly, are also featured as are travel luggage and gardening accessories. Bargains, on the other hand, can be hard to come by (this is, after all, the Côte d'Azur), although you can get lucky and make a very reasonable find.

WHEN TO GO ✤ HOW TO TRAVEL

This is one of the few parts of France where coming in the winter is actually a good idea (especially for North Americans and northern Europeans craving an escape from the cold). Flowers are in bloom year-round here, and lemon and orange trees are heavy with fruit during January and February. (Indeed, Menton's popular Fête du

Citron takes place in mid-February.) Winter daytime highs often reach the low 60s, and with abundant sunshine and protection from the wind it can feel positively balmy midday. Also, there are far fewer crowds in winter, a huge factor in this very busy region.

Of course, the fall and spring are especially glorious, with milder temperatures. By contrast, the summer is not only exceedingly crowded—often with lines of cars at the entrance and exit to towns—but also very hot, particularly at midday.

By far the easiest way to travel around is by train. A wonderful local rail system links up just about every community from Menton to Saint-Raphaël, with service several times a day. Most of the markets are within a few minutes' walk from the train station. A good bus system operates within the larger towns and between places that the train does not service. Driving here, on the other hand, is seriously stressful, with far too many cars and constant road repair mixed with aggressive, not terribly competent, drivers. Parking can also be difficult to find and expensive.

ANTIBES
*Thursday &
Saturday*

BOULEVARD D'AGUILLON
Thursday

Number of Vendors: 40 · Price-Quality: ⚜ ⚜ – ⚜ ⚜ ⚜
Scenic Value: ⚜ ⚜ – ⚜ ⚜ ⚜ · Amenities Nearby: ⚜ ⚜ ⚜ – ⚜ ⚜ ⚜

FEATURED ITEMS:

linens, paintings, ceramics, soda bottles, garden accessories,
glassware, copper pots, kitchenware generally

PLACE NATIONALE
Saturday

Number of Vendors: 25 · Price-Quality: ⚜ ⚜ ⚜ – ⚜ ⚜ ⚜ ⚜
Scenic Value: ⚜ ⚜ ⚜ · Amenities Nearby: ⚜ ⚜ ⚜ – ⚜ ⚜ ⚜

FEATURED ITEMS

linens, silver, paintings, carpets, regional ceramics,
Limoges boxes, well-polished tools, books

MARKET DETAILS

Antibes has two weekly flea markets. One is on Thursday along the boulevard d'Aguillon and the place J. Audiberti, on the edge of the *vieille ville*, just inside the walls near the port. The other is held on Saturday all day in the Place Nationale (and the place J. Audiberti) in the center of the old town. If arriving by car, the best option is to find parking along the side of the road near the port. It is a very short walk to both markets from there. If arriving by train, both markets are about a ten-minute walk from the station. Follow the avenue Robert Soleau south to the place Général de Gaulle, and then head east a few blocks on the rue de la République to the Place Nationale. The boulevard d'Aguillon is just a couple of blocks further east toward the *vieux port*.

ANTIBES, THOUGH JUST A FEW KILOMETERS WEST OF NICE, HAS AN ENTIRELY DIFFERENT FEEL, MUCH MORE REMINISCENT OF PROVENCE THAN THE CÔTE d'Azur. Perhaps that is because, for a few hundred years beginning in the fifteenth century, Antibes was a military post of the French kings, bordering the House of Savoy territories to the east. Unlike the brilliant pastels of Nice, the colors in this town are more muted, more neutral.

And while it lacks the dramatic and stunning setting of towns further east, Antibes is a very popular spot indeed, both with tourists and the well heeled. Just south of the center along the coast is the luxurious Cap d'Antibes, whose huge villas are hidden from the curious by tall hedges and parasol pines. Ironically, despite the evident wealth here (amply demonstrated by the many enormous yachts in the port), the atmosphere in this town is noticeably casual and relaxed, much more so than in other spots along the coast.

Antibes is one of those places that really grows on you, even if it does not bowl you over at first. Certainly, it has had that effect over the years on literary figures and other celebrities, like Graham Greene and Charlie Chaplin. The town has as its aesthetic center the harmonious plane tree–lined Place Nationale, from which radiate narrow streets filled with small boutiques, cafés and restaurants. It all feels very accessible, with much to offer visitors—the high-quality morning food market along the cours Masséna, the lively Thursday general market, the impressive Picasso museum by the sea, and the small, but sandy, public beach nearby.

BOULEVARD D'AGUILLON MARKET

Antibes's Thursday flea market by the ramparts is noticeably less high-brow than its Saturday counterpart in the Place Nationale. Here, just within the walls separating the town from the port, and spilling into the nearby square above, about 40 vendors set up their wares all day, coinciding with Antibes's large Thursday morning general market. Some of the vendors do not bother with attractive displays, content instead to simply pile their goods onto blankets on the ground, while others present their wares in a more appealing manner.

Though modest in size, this is a promising market for those hoping to make a good find. A friend who lives nearby and collects all sorts of things, including rustic green and mustard ceramics from Vallauris, paintings by local artists, linens and copper pots, swears by this market, though noting that it is very hit-and-miss. There is a wide variety in the kind and quality of goods here—lots of small decorative items, kitchenware, linens, silver, ceramics, glassware, etc.—and good turnover from one week to the next. The advantage is that if you find a treasure here you may be able to

purchase it at a very reasonable price (despite the fact that you found it in chic Antibes). But don't hesitate to bargain—vendors are used to it, and receptive.

PLACE NATIONALE MARKET

The Saturday flea market in the Place Nationale (and the place J. Audiberti) is a more upscale affair. The collectibles on offer in this spacious, shaded square are beautifully and carefully displayed. The 25 or so vendors here specialize in particular items—silver, ceramics, linens, rustic tools, paintings, books—and everything is well-polished and in pristine condition.

Don't expect to find a great bargain here, but for visitors without a lot of time, and interested in purchasing something of good quality, this is a market worth checking out. And, while not especially friendly, the vendors are accustomed to foreign buyers, and will likely be able to converse with you in English. Hard bargaining is perhaps frowned upon in this genteel scene, but asking for a modest reduction in the asking price is certainly permissible.

OTHER THINGS TO DO

The morning food market on the cours Masséna, very close to both flea markets, is one of the best in the Côte d'Azur, so try to leave some time to check it out. Here you can pick up wonderfully fresh vegetables and salad materials—like mesclun—as well as tapenade, seafood, ripe cheeses and fresh pasta. If the weather is nice, consider buying food for lunch here, and taking it to the beach just a minute away. Some of the many moderately priced restaurants here are a bit hit-and-miss, understandable given the touristy nature of this town.

Another place not to miss is Heidi's English Bookshop, just below the food market, at 24, rue Auberon, by the place J. Audiberti (tel. 04-93-34-74-11), where you will find a wide selection of both new and secondhand English books, a surprisingly scarce commodity in this region.

OTHER NEARBY MARKETS

The best nearby markets are featured separately in this chapter—the huge flea market in Nice on Mondays, Cannes's Saturday (and, twice a month, Sunday) market at Les Allées de la Liberté, and its Monday one in the Marché Forville. And, slightly further afield, and inland, is Valbonne's moderate-sized and pleasant market on the first Sunday of the month (except February and August).

CANNES

Saturday, first and
third Sunday of the
month & Monday

LES ALLÉES DE LA LIBERTÉ

Saturday, first and third Sunday of the month

Number of Vendors: 70 (Saturday), 40 (first and third Sunday of the month)

Price-Quality: ⚜ ⚜ ⚜ – ⚜ ⚜ ⚜ ⚜

Scenic Value: ⚜ ⚜ ⚜ · Amenities Nearby: ⚜ ⚜ ⚜ – ⚜ ⚜ ⚜ ⚜

FEATURED ITEMS

silver, porcelain, paintings, books, glassware, toys, vases, figurines

MARCHÉ FORVILLE

Monday

Number of Vendors: 60 · Price-Quality: ⚜ ⚜ ⚜ – ⚜ ⚜ ⚜

Scenic Value: ⚜ ⚜ ⚜ – ⚜ ⚜ ⚜ · Amenities Nearby: ⚜ ⚜ ⚜ – ⚜ ⚜ ⚜ ⚜

FEATURED ITEMS

tools, cameras, scientific/marine items, ceramics, linens, paintings,
posters, jewelry, toy soldiers, fashion accessories

MARKET DETAILS

Cannes has two *brocante* markets each week. One takes place all day on Saturday (and the first and third Sunday of the month) at Les Allées de la Liberté just across from the *vieux* port. The other is held all day on Monday at the Marché Forville, the market building at the corner of the rue du Marché Forville and the rue Louis Blanc (just a couple of minutes' walk up from the Les Allées market). If arriving by car, parking for both markets can be found in the covered lot just northwest of the Marché Forville. If arriving by train, both markets are just a ten-minute walk southwest from the station. For Les Allées, head south on the rue des Serbes, then turn right (west) on the rue d'Antibes, which leads to Les Allées de la Liberté (just west of the rue du Maréchal Joffre). For the Marché Forville, continue along the rue Félix Faure (the western extension of the rue d'Antibes), then turn right (north) on the rue Louis Blanc to the rue du Marché Forville.

THERE ARE STRONGLY DIVERGENT OPINIONS OF CANNES. SOME CONSIDER THIS A CHIC AND DESIRABLE PLACE TO BE, PARTICULARLY DURING THE FILM festival in May and in the summer when the city is jammed with vacationers. Others find the town disappointing—lacking both the spectacular setting and appealing center of other places along the coast, like Nice and Menton. Instead, they see shops that cater to the rich and beaches largely occupied by clients of the high-end hotels along La Croisette.

I actually like Cannes, particularly during the winter when it has the feel of a quiet but pleasant provincial city. Then, there is a friendly tone in the cafés and restaurants along the port and in the narrow streets of the old town, where distinctly unfashionable regulars meet to while away the hours. And, to satisfy any shopping cravings—

even just for window shopping—the expensive boutiques along the rue d'Antibes are fun to check out.

This is a town where English is often heard—spoken not just by tourists but by people who have settled here to live and work. Indeed, Cannes owes its growth, from small fishing village to tourist haven, to the English. During the 1830s, a British aristocrat, Lord Brougham, was forced to stop in Cannes because of a cholera epidemic further along the coast. He returned to set up winter residence here, and his example was then followed by other wealthy British citizens and later Russians, Germans and the Swiss. By the 1920s, Cannes had been transformed into a must-visit destination for the rich of Europe.

LES ALLÉES DE LA LIBERTÉ MARKET

On Saturday (and on the first and third Sunday of the month), a good-sized flea market takes place all day along the Allées de la Liberté, across from the *vieux* port. About 70 vendors (fewer on the first and third Sunday of the month) set up in this open space surrounded by plane trees, next to a lovely ornate gazebo. The setting, while not spectacular, is pleasing—you can spot the coast across the way, and take a break to watch the *boules* games nearby. On the other side of the market are several seafood restaurants, which spill onto the sidewalk when the weather is nice.

The quality of the wares at this market is generally high. Dealers tend to specialize in particular items—whether it is high-quality silver, crystal, Limoges boxes, old books, linens, canes or porcelain—and the prices are correspondingly moderately high to high. On the other hand, you will see a few vendors offering a variety of wares, either piled in boxes or spread out on the ground, and here you have a chance

of making quite a good find at a reasonable price. However, like Cannes itself, this is a market which consciously caters to tourists and foreigners and the prospect of real bargains is low. On the upside, though, if language is a barrier for you, several of the vendors will be able to communicate in English.

MARCHÉ FORVILLE MARKET

Cannes also has an indoor flea market, on Mondays, in the Marché Forville, just a couple of minutes' walk northwest of Les Allées de la Liberté. Serving other days as the site of Cannes's high-quality food market, on Mondays this spacious building, with its pleasing Art Deco features, is taken over by collectibles. About 60 or so vendors set up their tables along rows running the length of the building. The ambiance is low-key and pleasant, and the range of items both appealing and interesting, with prices generally more moderate than those at the more touristy outdoor market.

Here you will find paintings and posters, books and postcards, rustic tools and wooden items, porcelain and ceramics, toy soldiers, women's jewelry and accessories, and linens. Vendors are receptive to some bargaining and are well-accustomed to dealing with English-speaking visitors. Though this market is on a much smaller scale than Nice's giant Monday market, I would certainly recommend stopping by here as well, if time permits, or if getting to Nice on Monday does not fit into your plans.

OTHER THINGS TO DO

There are plenty of seafood restaurants to check out in the vicinity of both the Allées de La Liberté and Marché Forville markets. A little further afield, though, just off the rue d'Antibes, is a restaurant that serves refined food in a stylish setting, called

L'Affable (5, rue la Fontaine, tel. 04-93-68-02-09). Catering more to a business crowd than tourists, this spot's good-value lunch menu will not break the bank. Especially popular for dessert lovers are its soufflés.

For a lighter meal, or for very high-quality pastries, try Café Lenôtre (63, rue d'Antibes, tel. 04-97-06-67-65). And, if it is not Monday, be sure to take a stroll through the food market at the Marché Forville—one of the best I have been to in France, in terms of both the variety and quality of its produce.

OTHER NEARBY MARKETS

Nearby markets of interest are also featured in this chapter—Nice's large Monday market, Antibes's Thursday and Saturday markets, the market on the first Sunday of the month (except February and August) in Valbonne, and the all-day Sunday market outside Fréjus, along the coast west of Cannes.

FRÉJUS
Sunday

Number of Vendors: 100 · Price-Quality: ❧ – ❧ ❧
Scenic Value: ❧ · Amenities Nearby: ❧

FEATURED ITEMS

secondhand goods, kitchenware, tools, rustic items, garden accessories,
coins, Champagne capsules (the round piece atop the cork,
attached to the bottle with a wire), posters, books

MARKET DETAILS

This market takes place on Sunday from early in the morning to mid-afternoon in
a field about three kilometers from the center of Fréjus. If arriving by car, take
the Fréjus exit on the autoroute and follow signs to the center. You should see
notices marking the directions to the flea market along the road. The specific
address is chemin St. Joseph in Le Colombier, next to the Lorenzo *pépinière* (garden
center).

A FEW KILOMETERS FROM SAINT-RAPHAËL, JUST INLAND FROM THE COAST,
FRÉJUS IS A TOWN WITH A LONG HISTORY. ORIGINALLY A ROMAN NAVAL
base, its ancient past is still visible here and there as you drive through

town—in the remains of its walls and aqueduct, as well as its intact (and still utilized) arena.

As was the case in the past, modern-day Fréjus is more of a workaday town than its resort-like neighbor, Saint-Raphaël. There is also something a bit bucolic about this place, especially during the winter months when the *vieille ville*, with its impressive medieval center, feels quite deserted. Still, a drive through the countryside—the rocky red earth and scrubby terrain dotted with beautiful parasol pines—is very pleasing. It feels almost like a Mediterranean Wild West.

THE MARKET

The Sunday flea market which takes place a few kilometers outside of the center of town is a very down-home, unpolished affair, and a blunt reminder that not all is wealthy and pristine on the Côte d'Azur. In a large field, surrounded by gardening centers, around 100 vendors (seemingly regular people rather than dealers) set up shop here beginning very early on Sunday morning and lasting until mid-afternoon. You will find plenty of secondhand clothes, toys, books and electronic gear piled on blankets and even hanging from nearby trees. You will also see lots of everyday kitchenware (dishes, glassware, pots and pans and utensils). A few vendors specialize in particular collectibles—well-polished tools and garden implements, coins, Champagne capsules, linens and posters—but most focus on secondhand goods generally.

This is one market in this region that will appeal to intrepid bargain hunters willing to search through piles of unappealing junk to make a find. However, I would not recommend it to general tourists or those who prefer to keep a certain vision of France intact. If you do come, follow the example of dealers here and arrive early if you can. I found a few interesting pieces of old kitchenware at rock-bottom prices, so I was pleased. (I also bought a lovely hand-turned wooden bowl carved from alder and a pestle made from boxwood, carved by the vendor himself.) Be warned that the amenities here are very limited; while a small truck sells drinks and snacks, washroom facilities are scarce indeed.

OTHER THINGS TO DO

For sustenance after the flea market, a restaurant in Fréjus that garners favorable reviews, especially for its very fresh seafood, is Les Potiers (135, rue des Potiers, tel. 04-94-51-33-74). If you have a car, and a few hours to spend, consider taking the coastal road out of town instead of the autoroute. Surrounded by red rocky ridges and little peninsulas along the sea, it is one of the best drives in France.

OTHER NEARBY MARKETS

Saint-Raphaël has a small all-day flea market on Tuesday in the Place Coullet. There is also a moderate-sized all-day market on Wednesday in the town of Cogolin, not far from Saint-Tropez, at the Armée d'Afrique roundabout. And Saint-Tropez's wonderful general market, which takes place on Tuesday and Saturday mornings, also has several *brocante* vendors, selling high-quality and high-priced collectibles.

MENTON
Friday, second Sunday of the month

Number of Vendors: 20 to 25 · Price-Quality: ⚜ ⚜ ⚜
Scenic Value: ⚜ ⚜ ⚜ – ⚜ ⚜ ⚜ ⚜ · Amenities Nearby: ⚜ ⚜ ⚜ ⚜

FEATURED ITEMS

small decorative objects, silver, porcelain, glassware, colorful regional ceramics, paintings, books, women's clothing and accessories, travel and nautical items

MARKET DETAILS

The Menton flea market takes place all day on Friday and on the second Sunday of the month, between the Quai de Monléon and the Promenade du Soleil, just next to the Mediterranean. If arriving by car, look for free parking in the nearby port. If taking the train, it is about a 20-minute walk from the station. Head one block east to the Jardin Biovès and then south past the Casino to the seaside promenade, which leads a few blocks east to the market.

MENTON—IN MY VIEW BY FAR THE MOST BEAUTIFUL TOWN ON THE RIVIERA—IS THE SOUTHEASTERN-MOST POINT IN FRANCE, SMACK DAB UP AGAINST THE Italian border. Its setting is spectacular indeed, with rugged mountains framing the town and the beautiful green-blue Mediterranean forming an arc along its long beaches. The natural splendors are matched by the town itself, with brilliant pastel buildings edging the sea and the *basilique* Saint-Michel, with its pebble-decorated square, offering views of Italy to the east and Cap Martin to the west.

Like many places along the coast, Menton has a very Italian feel, for good reason. During its history, control of the town alternated between Italy and nearby Monaco until it reverted to France in 1860. For a few years during World War II, Menton was occupied by Italy, and in recent years, Italians have returned in droves, to purchase property or simply to spend weekends and holidays. The Italian presence is so great—along the promenade and in the pedestrian streets—that some locals claim that Menton is really an Italian town.

The British (as well as the Russians) have also had a long history here, wintering in Menton since the mid-nineteenth century. One of its most famous visitors at the time, Dr. James Bennett, touted the town's beneficial climate for the treatment of tuberculosis. The British are also credited with bringing exotic plants here and developing some of the area's renowned gardens. And, apart from the many varieties of trees and succulent plants, there are the lemon, orange, mandarin and grapefruit trees (and even a few bananas), all contributing to the town's (self-proclaimed, albeit justifiable) status as "*la perle de la France.*"

THE MARKET

Menton's flea market, which takes place all day Friday and the second Sunday of the month, is quite small with about 20 to 25 vendors (more on Sunday than Friday). It is held along the walkway between the town's elegant food market building and the sea. While the surroundings could hardly be more stunning, the immediate location of the market itself is a bit arid (by Menton standards).

Like so many of the flea markets in this region, this one features small decorative objects from France and from nearby Italy. Here you will find brilliantly colorful ceramics from Monaco and Vallauris and more rustic examples from Vallauris and Biot. Silver, including tableware from the cruise ships which toured the region, is featured, as well as porcelain and crystal. Women's clothing and accessories—scarves, purses, hats and vintage sunglasses—are popular, including fur coats (which Italian women wear in winter, despite the balmy temperatures).

Though small in size, the market offers some appealing collectibles—paintings and prints of life along the coast or perhaps vintage banners from the Carnaval de Nice. I have made some fun purchases here, including a porcelain brandy container in the shape of Corsica, with Napoleon's image emblazoned on it, for five euros, and a fluted ceramic bowl in earthy tones for ten. While I would not recommend traveling far out of your way to see this market, it is certainly well worth a quick visit on a sunny day.

OTHER THINGS TO DO

Menton is not blessed with great restaurants, unlike the Italian towns across the border. An exception, though, is Le Mirazur (30, avenue Aristide Briand, tel. 04-92-41-86-86), an elegant, modern spot with an extraordinary view, excellent food and attentive service. Located just next to the upper border with Italy on the eastern edge of town, and recently awarded its first Michelin star (as was the Hotel Paris-Rome, located on the seaside road below), this restaurant is expensive, but has a reasonably affordable lunch menu.

Near the other end of the culinary spectrum, very good wood-oven pizza can be had in the center of town at Vesuvio (19, place du Cap, tel. 04-93-57-29-83). And a very pleasant inexpensive place for lunch is the Menton tennis club (14, rue Albert 1er, tel. 04-93-57-85-85), near the train station, where you can eat outside next to the clay courts, surrounded by flowers and palm trees. It's a welcome oasis in this busy town.

For the more adventurous, a really special experience is to have lunch high in the mountains above Menton, at the Ferme St. Bernard (tel. 04-93-28-28-31), just beyond the village of Castellar. The owner will meet you in Castellar (perhaps in his ancient jeep) and drive you the last few kilometers up a rugged lane to his farm. The trip is a bit exciting (especially for those, like me, who do not relish winding steep roads with no siderails) but once there you will be very glad you came. Lunch is served in a rustic building with a giant open fireplace and the fare is simple but delicious—we had *barbajuan* (deep-fried dumplings filled with Swiss chard), eggplant gratin, ravioli and a fruit tart. After lunch, you can stroll along the paths nearby, surrounded by goats, sheep and horses. Perched among the mountain peaks with stunning views down to the sea, and no other buildings in sight, you would hardly believe that you are in the very crowded Côte d'Azur.

Menton is renowned for its lemons and a real specialty is the *limoncello* (the liqueur so popular here and in Italy) produced from organic lemons at the Citronneraie (tel. 04-93-35-43-43), just above the town near the entrance to the autoroute (heading in the direction of Genoa). The owner's lemons are renowned in France (he supplies some of the country's finest restaurants) and his lemon marmalade is also delicious. Be sure to call ahead before you come. If you are lucky, Monsieur Mazet (once a

Formula One driver) will also offer a tour of the orchard, where he has been cultivating lemons for 50 years.

If you really want good local cuisine, nearby towns in Italy are where to go for their renowned Ligurian cooking. The charming village of Dolceacqua, a few kilometers off the coast, between Ventimiglia and Bordighera, has a comfortable and very popular restaurant called Il Borgo (2, Salita San Sebastiano, tel. 39-0184-206-972), which serves great wood-fired pizzas and simple, delicious pasta (try anything with artichokes or porcini mushrooms). Just a few kilometers from Dolceacqua, the picturesque mountainside village of Apricale has a very fine, albeit formal, restaurant, Delio (9, Piazza Vittorio Veneto, tel. 39-0184-208-008) where sophisticated, Ligurian dishes are served in a dining room overlooking the surrounding hills.

For a great café experience (the coffee in Italy is much better than in France), try Caffè Vergnano 1882 (6, Via Chiappori) in the appealing workaday town of Ventimiglia, just across the border from Menton. (This is part of a small chain, with cafés in Nice and London, for example.) The décor is stylish, the cappuccino is excellent and the prices (at this location) are great.

OTHER NEARBY MARKETS

Apart from the other markets featured in this chapter, there is a small flea market on Saturday, all day, in nearby Monaco, at the port of Fontvieille.

NICE
Monday

Number of Vendors: 180 to 200 · Price-Quality: ❧❧-❧❧❧
Scenic Value: ❧❧❧❧ · Amenities Nearby: ❧❧❧❧

FEATURED ITEMS

silver, ceramics, paintings, kitchenware, cameras, phonographs,
advertising items, antique clothing and accessories, linens,
militaria, Art Deco, books, tools, toys

MARKET DETAILS

The Nice flea market is held all day on Monday (until mid-afternoon) along the
cours Saleya, and in the adjacent place Pierre Gauthier, parallel to and just north of
the Quai des États-Unis (the eastern extension of the Promenade des Anglais). If
arriving by car, the best bet is to park in the lot by the place Guynemer, a few hundred
meters farther east, by the port.

IF YOU ARE TRAVELING BY TRAIN, THE MARKET IS ABOUT A 20- TO 25-
MINUTE WALK SOUTHEAST OF NICE'S CENTRAL STATION. HEAD SOUTH ON AVENUE
Durante (and its continuation, rue du Congrès) until you reach the Promenade
des Anglais. Follow the promenade to the archway of the Quai des États-Unis.

Through here you will see the easternmost end of the market. (Another option is to jog a block north a few streets earlier, and turn right on the rue Saint-François-de-Paule, which leads into the cours Saleya from the west.)

To some, Nice marks the true beginning of the Côte d'Azur. Unlike Cannes and Antibes to the west, whose architecture is more Provençal and muted in tone, Nice is awash in beautiful pastel shades of yellow, orange, pink and green. It has a very Italianate feel, not surprising given that for almost 500 years Nice was under the control of the Italian House of Savoy, until its return to France in 1860. The British have also left a big mark here, most obviously in the building of the Promenade des Anglais in the early nineteenth century. But Nice's origins go much further back, to the Greeks, who named the town Nikea.

This is a city about which opinions are divided. Its detractors cite its busy traffic, petty crime and a history of corruption. Its promoters, on the other hand, have only to point to its extraordinary old center and its wonderful coastline, where people sunbathe and swim, even in January.

The most appealing section of town is certainly *vieux* Nice, a small area of winding, narrow streets edged by colorful centuries-old buildings. Its centerpiece is the cours Saleya, perhaps the most beautiful public space in the Côte d'Azur, lined with harmonious yellow, orange, pink and ochre structures. On most days of the week, this sunny oasis is host to a renowned food and flower market, but on Mondays it is the site of Nice's flea market.

THE MARKET

The Nice flea market, with between 180 and 200 vendors, is by far the largest in the Côte d'Azur and the one that offers the greatest variety in collectibles, as well as in prices. It is a favorite haunt of both general tourists and collectors, who join the throngs strolling along the rows of stalls, gazing at the wares, listening to live music and perhaps eating a slice of *socca* (a chickpea crêpe). At this market, you will hear English, German, Dutch, Swedish, Danish, Japanese and lots of Italian—among several other languages—as you walk along.

Collectors will be especially thrilled with this market. Here you can find just about anything—silver, glassware, porcelain, ceramics, linens, books, paintings, well-polished tools, *boules*, coffee grinders, Art Deco items, vintage clothing and accessories, posters, toys and some furniture. Given Nice's cosmopolitan past, you will not only find collectibles from all regions of France, but also from Europe and beyond. I am always excited when I spot old ceramics and glassware from the United States, for example.

Vendors at this market tend to concentrate on particular collectibles, but there are several who pile odds and ends on the ground (particularly in the place Pierre Gauthier) for people to rifle through. One of the great features here is the very good turnover in the wares; you see new and different things each time you come. One Monday, for example, you will notice several antique travel trunks, complete with compartments for all the accessories of nineteenth-century travel. The next week it may be old cannons and *jarres* (large ceramic containers), dredged up from the sea.

Not surprisingly, the prices of the well-polished items at the most beautifully arranged booths are quite high (particularly along the *cours* itself). But there are bargains to be had at this market—especially when it comes to collectibles from outside France and Italy—which is what makes it particularly interesting to collectors.

From every perspective, the Nice flea market is among the very best in France—right up there, for example, with the Porte de Vanves in Paris and the markets in Belfort, Annecy, Tours and Toulouse—and it has the added attraction of taking place in one of the most beautiful spots in France.

OTHER THINGS TO DO

If you want a nice lunch outside, alongside the market, a good spot is Le Safari (1, cours Saleya, tel. 04-93-80-18-44), noted for its fish and thin-crust pizza. For an indoor meal, a great spot, also close by, is L'Acchiardo (38, rue Droite, tel. 04-93-85-51-16) up one of the narrow streets leading off of the *cours*. Here, typical Niçois dishes—*farcis* (stuffed vegetables), pasta with pesto, *soupe de poisson*—are served in a rustic setting with beamed ceilings and walls lined with copper pots and old prints of the coast. Diners are served at long tables by the friendly staff, who are welcoming to locals and foreigners alike.

A somewhat more expensive restaurant, just a couple of minutes' walk from the western end of the market, is La Merenda (4, rue de la Terrasse). This tiny spot is deceptively basic. There is no telephone, the simple menu is written on the blackboard, and no credit cards are accepted. Yet the food, with a serious focus on local cuisine, is sophisticated and of high quality.

For a really inexpensive snack (though closed on Mondays), head to Chez René Socca (2, rue Miralhetti) in the old town. Having ordered one of their Niçoise specialties—*socca*, *pissaladière* (a thin pizza-like tart with anchovies) and stuffed vegetables, for example, you then sit down and eat at one of the picnic tables outside.

Also not open on Mondays, but a shop you must try to visit while you are in town, is L'Alziari (14, rue Saint-François de Paule, tel. 04-93-85-76-92). Alziari sells very fine quality olive oil produced at its mill nearby, olives and olive soaps (which last forever and also come in other wonderfully smelling varieties, like "tilleul" and lavender). Down the street, at number 7, check out Auer (tel. 04-93-85-77-98), an ornately decorated candy store featuring, among other treats, candied fruits (much revered in France).

OTHER NEARBY MARKETS

In addition to Antibes's Thursday and Saturday markets, Cannes's Monday and Saturday (and, twice-monthly, Sunday) markets, and the Villefranche-sur-Mer Sunday markets, the town of Beaulieu-sur-Mer, east of Villefranche, has a small all-day market by the port, on the first and third Sunday of the month.

VALBONNE
First Sunday
of the month, except
February and August

Number of Vendors: 40 to 50 · Price-Quality: ⚜ ⚜ ⚜
Scenic Value: ⚜ ⚜ ⚜ · Amenities Nearby: ⚜ ⚜ – ⚜ ⚜ ⚜

FEATURED ITEMS

ceramics, glassware, linens, books, paintings, decorative items,
silver, jewelry, some furniture

MARKET DETAILS

The Valbonne flea market is held all day on the first Sunday of the month (except in February and August). The market takes place in the center of town, along the rue du Cours and in the place des Arcades, the main square in the heart of the village.

VALBONNE IS A CHARMING VILLAGE SET IN THE *ARRIÈRE PAYS* BETWEEN NICE AND GRASSE. IT OFFERS A VERY WELCOME RESPITE FROM THE HECTIC scene along the coast, particularly during the busy summer months. While there are certainly plenty of tourists and foreigners to be found here, Valbonne is more reminiscent of the out-of-the-way villages of Provence than of the flashy Riviera. The town itself is quite small, consisting of a few narrow streets radiating

from the central square—the place des Arcades—which is lined with centuries-old, arched passageways. It is evident from the well-maintained stone buildings and freshly-painted shutters that the town has been gentrified, no doubt partly in response to the influx of foreigners who have purchased second homes in the vicinity. Yet, unlike some places where outsiders seem to rob towns of their character, Valbonne has a positive, albeit international feel—perhaps not altogether French, but a harmonious blend of French and other nationalities. On a recent visit, I was struck by the number of couples, with children in tow, where one of the parents was French and the other was not.

THE MARKET

Valbonne's monthly flea market (on the first Sunday of the month, except in February and August) takes place all day in the place des Arcades and adjoining streets. About 50 vendors set up their wares here, offering a wide selection of antiques and collectibles. Regional ceramics, including pottery from Vallauris and nearby Provence, and *jarres* from Biot, are a big feature. Linens, silver, jewelry, paintings and posters are also much in evidence.

Prices here are moderate to moderately high. One gets the impression that this has something to do with the clientele of well-heeled property owners nearby. (The abundance of well-polished rustic furniture lends support to this notion.) Bargain hunters will likely not make a great find, but this is a pleasant market to visit nonetheless, especially for those looking for a congenial outing on a sunny day.

OTHER THINGS TO DO

If the weather permits, a good idea is to sit down for lunch at the Café des Arcades (tel. 04-93-12-00-06), which shares the square with the flea market. While service can be very slow, the food is good and reasonably priced, and it is hard to beat the setting of this sunny oasis. After lunch, if you have time, visit the nearby town of Biot, with its many boutiques selling ceramics and glassware. In the center of the village there is a tastefully-decorated and comfortable *salon de thé* called Le Mas des Orangers (3, rue des Roses, tel. 04-93-65-18-10).

OTHER NEARBY MARKETS

If you are staying in the area, the town of Vence has a small all-day flea market on the third Sunday of the month, in the place du Maréchal Juin, as well as a modest-sized all-day Wednesday market, at the place du Grand Jardin.

VILLEFRANCHE-
SUR-MER
Sunday

QUARTIER DE L'OCTROI
Sunday

Number of Vendors: 20 · Price-Quality: ⚜ ⚜ ⚜
Scenic Value: ⚜ ⚜ · Amenities Nearby: ⚜ ⚜ – ⚜ ⚜ ⚜

FEATURED ITEMS

porcelain, glassware, vases, paintings and prints, books, some furniture

PLACE A. POLLONNAIS
Sunday

Number of Vendors: 30 · Price-Quality: ⚜ ⚜ – ⚜ ⚜ ⚜
Scenic Value: ⚜ ⚜ ⚜ – ⚜ ⚜ ⚜ ⚜ · Amenities Nearby: ⚜ ⚜ ⚜

FEATURED ITEMS

silver, jewelry, porcelain, paintings, glassware,
small decorative items generally

MARKET DETAILS

There are two all-day flea markets on Sunday in Villefranche-sur-Mer—one at the Quartier de l'Octroi, along the Basse Corniche at the top end of town, and the other in the place A. Pollonnais, in the lower part by the sea.

I F YOU HAVE A CAR, PARKING FOR THE QUARTIER DE L'OCTROI MARKET CAN BE FOUND IN A SMALL LOT JUST EAST OF THE MARKET, ALONG THE CORNICHE, while parking for the place A. Pollonnais is available in the lot in the lower part of town. If arriving by train, both markets are within easy walking distance from the station. Villefranche-sur-Mer is one of the most picturesque towns along the Côte d'Azur. Nestled in the bay between the peninsula of Cap Ferrat and the environs of Nice, its setting could hardly be more striking, and the town itself, with its colorful old buildings descending to the charming port, completes the picture.

This is also a very touristy place, visited in droves by both land and sea. The deep waters of the bay allow large cruise ships to stop here, as they regularly do, disgorging their passengers for lunch by the water or a stroll through town.

Yet Villefranche manages to retain its charms. It is one of the best places along the coast for sitting outside—at one of its several cafés and restaurants—taking in the sun and observing the scene. And, if that's not enough activity, you can always visit its pristine, medieval Chapelle de Saint-Pierre, decorated in the late 1950s by Jean Cocteau, in pastel strokes depicting images of Saint Peter, fishermen (with fish-shaped eyes) and gypsies.

QUARTIER DE L'OCTROI MARKET

At the smaller, and less scenic, of Villefranche's two Sunday flea markets, in the Quartier de l'Octroi (along the Basse Corniche), you will find about 20 vendors set up alongside the road and in the adjacent garden. Despite its less-than-stellar setting, this is a high-end and high-quality market, featuring mostly decorative items like silver, porcelain, glassware and paintings, including works by local artists. Prices are moderately high to high; this is not a spot where you are likely to make a great find, unbeknownst to the quite savvy and knowledgeable dealers.

PLACE A. POLLONNAIS MARKET

More substantial than its counterpart above, the place A. Pollonnais market is located in a much more appealing spot—right by the water in the area in front of the legendary Welcome Hotel. Here, about 30 vendors set up shop all day on Sunday, offering a wide range of items—mostly decorative goods, like silver, porcelain and glassware, but also functional collectibles (baskets, linens, tools, wooden items) in good condition and at fairly steep prices. You will also find a lot of jewelry here. The most surprising item I spotted, the last time I came, was a giant, elaborately carved elephant tusk, perhaps a meter long.

Among the dealers selling expensive and high-end goods are a few offering more everyday, and reasonably-priced, collectibles, making this a market of at least some interest for bargain hunters, as well as collectors with deeper pockets.

OTHER THINGS TO DO

After browsing the markets, take a break at one of the cafés and restaurants alongside the water. One place I like (despite its somewhat corny décor) is Trastevere

(7, quai Amiral Courbet, tel. 04-93-01-94-26), where the *moules avec frites* are good and reasonably priced (and can be happily washed down with a cool bottle of rosé).

If you have time, I highly recommend a quick visit to the hilltop town of Eze, along the Moyenne Corniche. Its lovely Château Eza (rue de la Pise, tel. 04-93-41-12-24) has a stunning cliffside *terrasse*; though even just a drink here is similarly steep, this is perhaps the most breathtaking spot along the Côte d'Azur, and well worth the price.

OTHER NEARBY MARKETS

Just a few kilometers further east along the Basse Corniche is the striking town of Beaulieu-sur-Mer, which has a small, high-end flea market on the first and third Sunday of the month, all day, alongside the port.

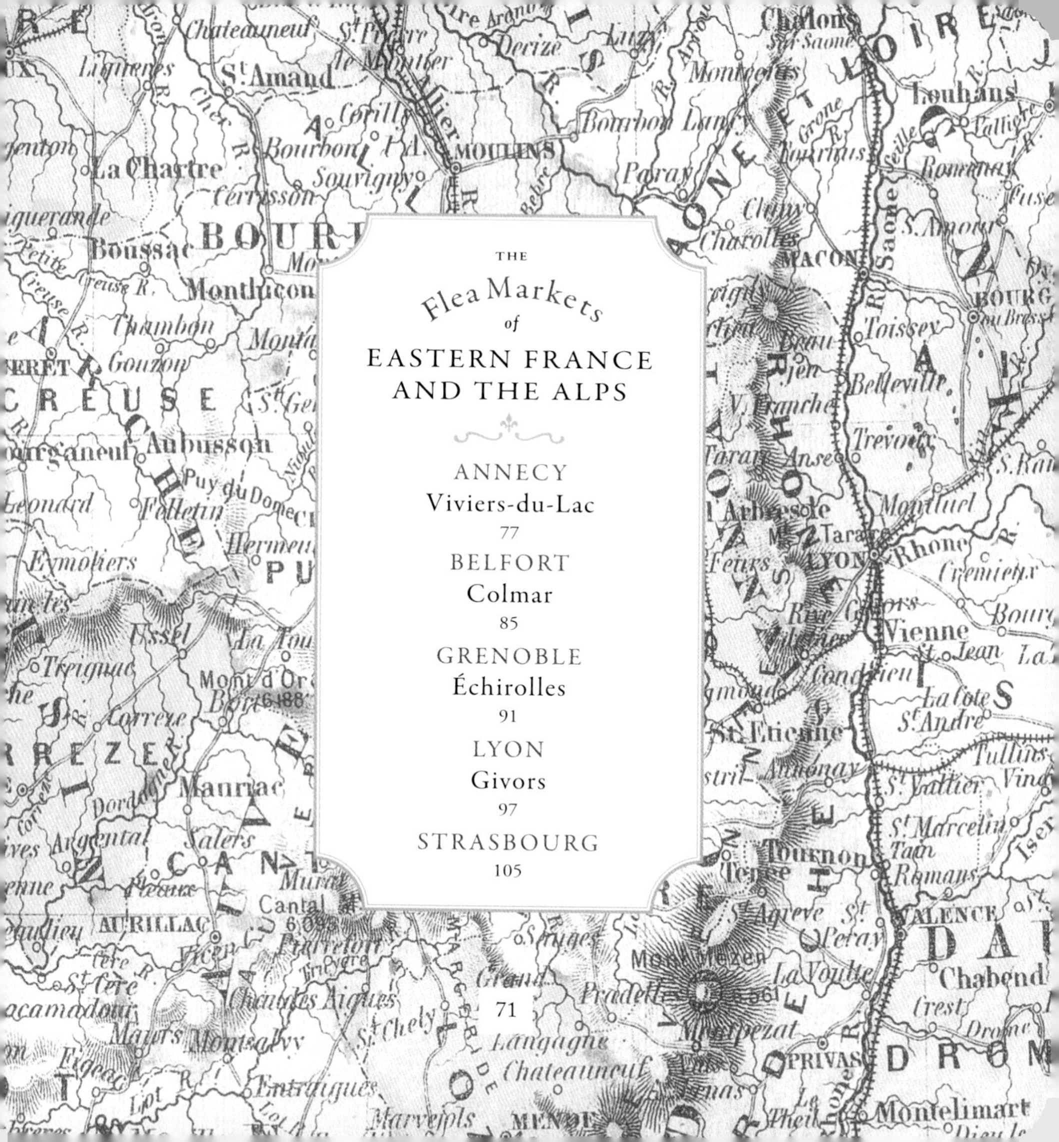

THE

Flea Markets of EASTERN FRANCE AND THE ALPS

THE

Flea Markets

of

EASTERN FRANCE
AND THE ALPS

❧

ABOUT THE REGION

THE SECTION OF FRANCE EAST FROM LYON AND NORTH FROM GRENOBLE IS ONE OF THE MOST BEAUTIFUL PARTS OF THE COUNTRY, THOUGH IT DOES not perhaps command as much interest for visitors as places like Provence and the Côte d'Azur. In addition to Lyon (just below the southern edge of Burgundy), it embraces the splendid Alps, their valleys dotted with tiny villages, the picturesque towns of Alsace with their colorful, half-timbered buildings, and the mysterious Franche-Comté, with the forests and plateaus of the Jura mountains. This is a region deeply marked by its terrain and its rural character. There is a wonderful feeling of space here, which one can quickly crave after spending just a few days in Paris, or on the Côte d'Azur, for example.

The rustic, rural nature of much of this region is reflected in the solid architecture of its buildings, and in the heartiness of its cuisine. Lyon, the gastronomic heart of France, is renowned (*nouvelle cuisine* aside) for its cheeses, sausages and fresh produce, and for its wonderfully casual *bouchons*, the small restaurants noted for their convivial atmosphere and bracing fare. A similarly hearty quality is reflected in the *choucroutes* and *tartes flambées* (pizza-like tarts, with cream, onions and bacon) of Alsace, and the fondues, *raclettes* and *tartiflettes* (melted cheese over cream and potatoes) of the Savoie and Alps regions. There is little danger of leaving the table hungry here.

ABOUT THE MARKETS

That solid, bracing quality also characterizes the collectibles found in the flea markets in this part of France. Here, you will find a marked emphasis on rustic items and everyday collectibles—tools, solid wooden armoires and trunks, wooden utensils and implements, ceramic foie gras and mustard containers, functional ceramics, skis and snowshoes, cowbells and implements for making milk, butter and cheese. Even the paintings here often depict hearty mountain scenes. I particularly love the ceramics—from the Savoie, those so-simple yet graceful milk pitchers, decorated with polka dots, squiggles, mountain flowers and swirls (a marble effect called *jaspe*). And from Alsace, in addition to earthenware pitchers and bowls with primitive flowers and simple geometric patterns, you will see functional stoneware jugs with blue blotches, and *kugelhopf* (a round Alsatian cake), or lamb-shaped, baking molds. You will also see wine collectibles, enamel plaques and old clocks, reflecting the economic activities that have long animated this corner of France.

The character of the flea markets also mirrors the solidity of the region. Perhaps not surprisingly, there are fewer here than in the area further south, but the ones that do exist are well-established and substantial—the Villeurbanne market (on the edge of Lyon), for example, is one of the largest in France. The monthly Annecy and

Belfort markets are also very impressive, in terms of both their setting and the variety of their wares. While the monthly collectibles market in Grenoble is on a much smaller scale, it offers interesting bargain-hunting when combined with other nearby markets, like the one in Sassenage. Strasbourg's market, though also of modest size, has the advantage of being held twice a week. And, despite its small size, it offers an interesting glimpse at the collectibles of the region. You will feel, once you have scoured the flea markets here, that you have gained real insight into everyday life in this appealing corner of France.

WHEN TO GO ❧ HOW TO TRAVEL

Given the often chilly winters, it is best to come in the late spring, summer or early fall, if possible. Indeed, the not-to-be-missed Belfort market is not held in January or February, and Annecy's market is reduced in size then. In the warmer months, the markets are not only larger but also much more lively and animated. This is one region where visiting during the summer can be quite pleasant, as it is not oppressively hot.

While you can take the train to most of the markets in this region, train routes can be slow, particularly if you are not departing from Paris. Also, given its rural focus and the beauty of the natural surroundings, this is a part of France in which having a car will give you far better access to its charms. In addition, you will experience much less congestion on the roads, not to mention stress, than in other regions, making the prospect of driving more palatable.

ANNECY
Last Saturday of the month

Number of Vendors: 120 to 170 · Price-Quality: ⚜ ⚜ ⚜ – ⚜ ⚜ ⚜ ⚜
Scenic Value: ⚜ ⚜ ⚜ – ⚜ ⚜ ⚜ ⚜ · Amenities Nearby: ⚜ ⚜ ⚜ ⚜

FEATURED ITEMS

Savoyard ceramics and furniture, skis, snowshoes,
farming tools, cowbells, cheese-making implements, coffee mills,
dolls, toys, paintings, linens, books, silver

MARKET DETAILS

Annecy's flea market takes place on the last Saturday of the month, all day. It is held in the old quarter, in the rue de l'Isle and its continuation, the rue Sainte-Claire, on the south side of the Canal du Thiou. In busy months, the market also extends to the other side of the Canal. If arriving by car, look for parking in one of the lots on the edge of the old quarter. If arriving by train, the market is about a ten-minute walk southeast of the station. Upon exiting, head south on the rue de la Gare across the canal, jogging a little east to the place Sainte-Claire. The market begins here.

IT IS HARD TO FIND A MORE BEAUTIFUL TOWN IN FRANCE THAN ANNECY. ITS SETTING IS MAGICAL—NESTLED AT THE WESTERN EDGE OF THE IMPOSSIBLY turquoise-colored Lac d'Annecy, ringed with snow-capped mountains. The old town with its narrow pedestrian and arcaded streets exudes charm, enhanced by the canal system which meanders through it. The canal is edged on both sides with appealing pastel buildings, decorated with overflowing flower boxes. Swans and ducks swim leisurely in the gentle waters of the canal and in the lake beyond. The air is fresh and crisp, as one would expect of a mountainous region far from major industrial sites.

This is a busy and energetic place. On weekends, its cafés and restaurants are filled with locals and visitors. Its lakeside park is packed with young families, playing soccer, flying kites, walking, running and cycling. The lake is dotted with people sailing, rowing and canoeing, even during the winter. And, of course, the mountains are right nearby, for hiking, skiing and para-jumping.

This is the wonderful Savoie region of France, with its picturesque Alpine farmhouses and cattle grazing on brilliantly green hillside pastures, with rugged mountains behind. Like the landscape and the architecture, the cuisine is hearty and robust. Cheese (tomme de Savoie, beaufort, reblochon) in all of its forms is a staple, in the Savoyard dishes of fondue, *raclette*, *tartiflette*, and *salade Savoyarde*. After just a few days here, one cannot help feeling reinvigorated and reconnected to nature, as well as stuffed.

THE MARKET

Annecy's monthly flea market, held all day on the last Saturday of the month, is one of the best in France and one of my favorites. Though it has shrunk somewhat over the last ten years (with often 120 vendors, as opposed to 170, though summer is busier), it is a very substantial market. It also offers a varied, and high-quality, range of collectibles. The market is held in the arcaded pedestrian area of the old town, and along the bridges that crisscross the Canal du Thiou. The setting is spectacular, particularly on a clear day when the canal is at its best and the streets are warmed by the glow of the sun.

Altogether apart from its scenic appeal, this is also a very interesting and impressive flea market. There is a marked concentration on the Savoie and Savoyard collectibles, although many vendors sell items from other parts of France. You will find the wonderfully simple, and yet so pleasing, Savoyard ceramics—bowls, milk jugs, and plates, decorated with polka dots, squiggles or tiny Alpine flowers, in pale yellow, brown, rust and green. You will also see ceramics in the signature *jaspe* style—where the glaze produces a marbled effect. Several years ago these ceramics were hard to come by and expensive. While not cheap, my impression is that prices have recently moderated somewhat, although it is still hard to find interesting pieces in good condition.

Several other Savoyard collectibles are featured here, as well—sculpted wooden butter molds, butter churns, cheesemaking items, carved wooden kitchen utensils, cow bells, agricultural implements, wooden shoes, paintings of Alpine scenes, skis, sleds, ice skates, snow shoes, fishing gear and large copper pots. There is also a lot of furniture in this market, including beautifully carved and painted wooden chests and armoires. While the emphasis is on rustic and rural items, you will also see toys (albeit often related to the farm, like old metal farm animals), linens, glassware, coffee mills, enamelware and glassware.

This is a friendly market where vendors are helpful and informative, and willing to bargain. On a recent visit a number confided that they thought the market had suffered somewhat in recent years, and that concern has perhaps been reflected in a moderation in prices and a greater willingness to negotiate. I purchased two small Savoyard plates for two and eight euros each—one polka-dotted, the other in the *jaspe* pattern—which I thought was very reasonable. This is a market I would strongly recommend to both general visitors and collectors, for its combination of size, variety, scenic value and fine Savoyard collectibles.

OTHER THINGS TO DO

Annecy has several restaurants to choose from, but many are geared to the tourist trade and are not considered particularly special or noteworthy. One place I really like—and a favorite of the locals—is Le Fréti (12, rue Sainte-Claire, tel. 04-50-51-29-52), located right alongside the flea market in the arcaded pedestrian street of the old town. This restaurant, devoted to cheese dishes—*raclette*, *tartiflette*, and many varieties of fondue—is above a shop selling giant rounds of wonderful regional cheeses. If you order *raclette*, a metal rack with a large piece of *raclette* cheese is placed on your table, with a heater next to it for melting. The fondue is served in large enamel pots for diners to dip into. The food is delicious, the atmosphere is relaxed and friendly, and you will leave feeling well-fortified and satisfied.

If you have a car (and an adventurous spirit), I strongly recommend a drive to La Ferme de la Charbonnière (route de Thônes, Menthon-Saint-Bernard, tel. 04-50-02-82-59), situated very close to the tiny village of Bluffy, on the eastern side of the lake, about a 15-minute drive from Annecy. Eating here will be one of the most

remarkable (meaning surprising) experiences of your culinary life, not just your trip to France. This is about as close to the farm as you can get; rough wooden tables and benches are set right in the barn, suspended above several dozen cows (chained, it must be said). Hanging cowbells line the hallway leading to the restaurant. Customers sit at the long tables and are served (in a rather unceremonious manner) simple and delicious Savoyard food. This is no-nonsense, "local fare" personified. A hearty loaf of bread is placed directly on the table, to eat along with your main course and cheese; once you have had your fill of the delicious cheeses, the wooden serving board is sent on to the next table. If it is any consolation to cow-lovers, beef is not on the menu—instead, there is *raclette*, fondue, *tartiflette*, and Savoyard salad. This is not a low-fat experience. After you have consumed your main course cheese dish, followed by cheese, you cannot imagine ever eating cheese again (and yet you wish you'd had more of it, it was so good). This is a very popular spot, the parking lot filled with cars on a Saturday night, for example, so book ahead.

Those who prefer a more pristine eating environment might wish to try L'Auberge des Dents de Lanfon (Col de Bluffy, tel. 04-50-02-82-51), very close by. Also set in this idyllic area just above Lac Annecy, this place has undergone a dramatic transformation in the last few years. What was before cozy and rustic has become chic and modern, with leather seats and white porcelain plates replacing the wooden chairs and Savoyard ceramics of the past (though some of the lovely old pots still decorate the walls). The food is similarly modern and sophisticated. I have to confess that I was disappointed in the transformation of the place, but I can understand that some may welcome a respite from rustic surroundings and high-fat food.

For those interested in Savoyard ceramics, a visit to the Fabriques des Poteries

Savoyardes studio, shop and museum in Évires (tel. 04-50-62-01-90) should be a priority. The driven, but also hospitable, proprietor, Jean-Christophe Hermann, has been producing high-quality wood-fired traditional milk jugs, bowls and other pieces for many years, and has also amassed an astonishing collection of antique regional ceramics dating from the twelfth century. The problem is in finding the shop and museum open. (It is closed from the beginning of November to Easter, and is otherwise open by appointment, so be sure to call ahead.) On a recent trip, I could not find M. Hermann's work for sale in Annecy, where the boutiques offer less traditional, and in my view much less appealing, pieces. I am told, though, that M. Hermann comes to the Annecy flea market very early each month, scouting for new additions to his collection.

OTHER NEARBY MARKETS

There are not a lot of regular flea markets in the vicinity of Annecy. If you are heading south from here, there is a *marché aux puces* on Sundays, all day, in Viviers-du-Lac, north of Chambéry, in the parking lot of the Intermarché store. And, in Chambéry itself, there is a small *brocante* market on the second Saturday of the month, all day, in the places Saint-Léger and Hôtel de Ville, as well as a *marché aux puces* on Sunday morning, in the parking lot of the Carrefour store, in the Chamnord shopping center.

BELFORT
First Sunday morning of the month, except January and February

Number of Vendors: 140 · Price-Quality: ⚜ ⚜ ⚜ – ⚜ ⚜ ⚜ ⚜
Scenic Value: ⚜ ⚜ ⚜ · Amenities Nearby: ⚜ ⚜ ⚜

FEATURED ITEMS

Alsatian ceramics and baking molds, enamel advertising plaques, clocks, skis, snowshoes, copper and brass ware, pewter, chocolate molds, dolls, linens, Art Deco items, toys, silver, trunks and luggage, paintings, militaria

MARKET DETAILS

Belfort's flea market is held on the first Sunday morning of the month, except January and February. The market takes place in the old quarter, in the place d'Armes (by the City Hall) and in nearby streets. If arriving by car, head for the *vieille ville*, in the center of town, east of the Savoureuse River. If arriving by train, turn left on the avenue Wilson as you exit the station, then go to your right (northeast) on the pedestrian Faubourg de France, which becomes the boulevard Carnot as it crosses the river. Skirt the southern edge of the place de la République, on the rue des Nouvelles, which leads to the place d'Armes.

BELFORT IS A SMALL CITY IN THE FRANCHE-COMTÉ REGION OF FRANCE, BETWEEN THE JURA MOUNTAINS TO THE SOUTH AND THE VOSGES TO THE north. The location has proven historically significant in the military struggles for control of this region. During the Franco-Prussian war, Belfort managed to resist a long siege by Prussian forces, thus avoiding the fate suffered by most of Alsace-Lorraine—annexation by Germany (which lasted until the end of the First World War and was repeated during the Second). The town's nineteenth-century military savior, Colonel Denfert-Rochereau, was known as the "lion of Belfort" and is commemorated by a giant statue of a lion which looks out over the city. (The statue was created by Bartholdi, who designed the Statue of Liberty, and who was born in Colmar, not far away.) The other significant vestiges of Belfort's military past are the giant fortress and fortifications built by Vauban, the French master of fort construction.

The city of Belfort is divided into two parts—the newer commercial center located on the west side of the Savoureuse River and the old town to the east. The commercial heart is of little interest to tourists (who are likely to bypass Belfort altogether, in favor of picturesque Colmar and its surrounding villages, about an hour away). However, the old center is quite appealing, with colorful imposing buildings lining the narrow streets leading off the place de la République and the place d'Armes.

THE MARKET

While Belfort does not itself present a big draw for visitors, its flea market in the *vieille ville* certainly does. Held on the first Sunday morning of the month (except in January and February) in and around the place d'Armes, this is one of the most significant and impressive flea markets in France, in size, variety and quality.

Approximately 140 vendors begin to set up their wares here early in the morning, well before it is light. Before they have come close to fully unwrapping their goods, dealers and curious collectors armed with flashlights have already arrived, to get first crack at the merchandise. As the morning advances they are joined by crowds of more general customers—especially mid-morning, when families with children in tow stroll along the narrow streets.

This is a market with a serious focus on regional collectibles from across northeast France—Alsace, Lorraine and Franche-Comté. You will find ceramic jugs and bowls with the classic Alsatian motifs—little flower patterns and geometric designs, in the signature shades of pale yellow, rust, brown and green, many produced in and around the town of Soufflenheim, north of Strasbourg. You will also see the classic Alsatian ceramic baking molds—a circular one with a point in the middle for making the signature *kugelhopf* cake, as well as molds shaped like lambs for special occasions. Several of the vendors also offer gray stoneware jugs with blue blotches, from Betschdorf, north of Soufflenheim. And from Lorraine, you will see many examples of the folkloric dishware produced in Sarreguemines.

Another collectible with a regional focus at this market is clocks—giant intact grandfather clocks, but also clock faces and parts—many of which come from in and around Besançon (in Franche-Comté, southwest of Belfort), a center for clock-making in France. You will also see Alsatian linens, chocolate molds, enamel plaques (a primary manufacturer was an Alsatian company), old ceramic foie gras containers

and mustard pots (from the area around Dijon, in neighboring Burgundy). Military collectibles are also popular, no doubt a reflection of Belfort's strategic past, as are carved wooden items, skis and snowshoes. And, of course, there are general collectibles of all kinds—books, toys, pewter, silver, glassware and copperware.

This is also a high-quality market, where prices are generally moderately high, although some interesting finds can be made. Vendors know what they are selling, but while many focus on certain collectibles whose value they are keenly aware of, there are a few offering odds and ends, piled in boxes on the ground, where you may find a good deal. In addition to French, German is commonly spoken by both customers and dealers (the license plates on cars in the vicinity indicate that a fair number come from nearby Switzerland and southern Germany). I have never heard English spoken here, which may suggest that this market is not yet on the Anglo tourism circuit—a shame because this is a really fine flea market, which offers a rare opportunity to find some of the most sought-after collectibles from this part of France.

OTHER THINGS TO DO

For a coffee or light snack right by the market, head to Aux Trois Maillets or the bakery/*salon de thé*, L. Francois, both in the place d'Armes. (Try the Alsatian pastry, *kugelhopf*, to boost your energy until lunch.) Otherwise, after seeing the market, I suggest heading for Colmar, which can be reached by train in just over an hour. (If you have a car, and some time, also check out the charming, albeit very touristy, nearby villages of Riquewihr and Kaysersberg, the birthplace of Albert Schweitzer.)

Though also inundated with tourists, and almost cloyingly picturesque, Colmar is a beautiful place, with wonderful examples of Alsatian architecture. For a good, reasonably priced meal—at a popular spot with the locals—try À La Ville de Paris (4, place Jeanne d'Arc, tel. 03-89-24-53-15), with its half-timbered exterior and comfortable dining room. (This kind of casual eatery is called a *winstub* in Alsace.) For a light snack, tea or coffee, an appealing and relaxing oasis is Au Croissant Doré (28 rue des Marchands) near the cathedral and opposite the Maison Pfister. This *salon de thé*, with its pink art nouveau exterior, is filled with collectibles, and run by a nice older woman. The experience will make you feel you are having a quiet visit with your favorite aunt.

OTHER NEARBY MARKETS

There are not many regular flea markets in the vicinity of Belfort. However, the town of Colmar has a small, all-day flea market on Friday, in the place des Dominicains.

GRENOBLE
Last Sunday of the month, except December

Number of Vendors: 60 to 80 · Price-Quality: ❧ ❧
Scenic Value: ❧ ❧ · Amenities Nearby: ❧ ❧

FEATURED ITEMS

Secondhand goods, kitchenware, copperware, toys, linens, tools

MARKET DETAILS

There are a number of regular flea markets in and around Grenoble. One takes place in Sassenage, just a few kilometers west of the center of Grenoble, on the last Sunday of the month (except December), in the parc Sasso Marconi. If arriving by car, head to the center of Sassenage and follow the signs which you will see posted.

WHILE MANY ASSOCIATE GRENOBLE WITH MOUNTAINS AND ALPINE SKIING, THIS IS ACTUALLY A SUBSTANTIAL CITY—AND THE ECONOMIC center of the Alps region of France—noted for its chemical, electronics and nuclear industries. It is also an intellectual center, its university dating from the fourteenth century. Accessible in about three hours from Paris by TGV (the

high-speed train), this is a modern, forward-looking place, with wide avenues, tall buildings and a good tramway system.

The mountainous area around Grenoble is its most impressive feature and perhaps presents a bigger draw for visitors than the city itself. If you have arrived in town from the south, around Gap, on one of the winding secondary roads, you have had a thrilling experience indeed, with snow-capped peaks and village-dotted valleys accompanying your journey.

Though much of Grenoble is too modern to be truly appealing, the old quarter is pleasant with large café-filled squares—for example, the place Grenette, the place de Gordes and the place Saint-André. And the rose-filled Jardin de Ville provides a romantic oasis on a sunny warm day.

THE MARKET

On my most recent trip to Grenoble, I decided to check out the flea market on the last Sunday of the month in Sassenage. This small community just a few kilometers west of the center of Grenoble is not beautiful, but it is pleasant enough, with high cliffs behind. The market, held in the small parc Sasso Marconi, is a modest, relaxed affair. The scene is casual, drawing nearby residents who come to check out the wares—mostly secondhand items (clothes, linens, toys, kitchenware), but with a few interesting collectibles mixed in.

About 60 to 80 vendors set up in this small space, mostly piling their goods on blankets on the ground. A few focus on collectibles (rustic items mostly, including copperware and old tools) but any discoveries you make will likely be well hidden under the used, practical goods that most of the customers have come to buy. While there is just a modest hope of finding something interesting, if you do, it will be inexpensive. I was happy with my purchase here—a white porcelain soup tureen for just one euro.

OTHER THINGS TO DO

After seeing the Sassenage market, you will want to head back to the old center of Grenoble. For a light snack, or a pleasant café experience, head for the place Grenette, the place de Gordes, or the place Saint-André—the first is the mostly lively, with the best crowd-watching potential, the second is more intimate and offers reasonable possibilities for eating and the third is where you will find the Café de la Table Ronde (7, place Saint-André, tel. 04-76-44-51-41), opened in 1739.

OTHER NEARBY MARKETS

The city of Grenoble has a moderate-sized collectibles market, all day on the first Saturday of the month (except August), in and around the place André Malraux. The setting is not the most scenic, as the place Malraux is modern (as is the imposing Chambre de Commerce et de l'Industrie nearby). The last time I was here I noticed that the dealers tend to specialize in particular collectibles—paintings, silver, glassware, books, linens, well-polished rustic items, high-quality kitchenware (ceramics, copper pots and coffee mills)—and that the prices are correspondingly moderately high.

Grenoble also has two very down-home weekly flea markets, both on Sunday morning. The first takes place in the parking lot of the Intermarché store, north of the center of town, across the Isère River; the market is just northwest of the place

Aristide Briand, off the avenue de l'Esplanade. The second market is in the Atac parking lot along the rue Stalingrad, south of the place A. Malraux.

To the southwest of Grenoble, the community of Échirolles also has a Sunday morning flea market, in the parking lot of the Bricolage warehouse, in the espace Comboire. And Sassenage has a second monthly market, held on the first Sunday of the month, in the parc de l'Ovalie, halle J. Longo.

LYON
Sunday morning

Number of Vendors: 400 · Price-Quality: ✤ ✤ – ✤ ✤ ✤
Scenic Value: ✤ – ✤ ✤ · Amenities Nearby: ✤ – ✤ ✤

FEATURED ITEMS

furniture, farm implements, tools, kitchenware, ceramics, paintings, dolls, linens, pewter, boules, rustic items generally

MARKET DETAILS

A huge flea market takes place on Sunday morning on the outskirts of Lyon northeast of the city center, in Villeurbanne. Getting here by car can be complicated, and depends on the direction you are coming from. The best thing to do is get a detailed map of the area and plot your route to Villeurbanne from there. The market is located at 1 route du Canal, alongside the Canal de Jonage (a sign, with the words Canal des Puces, marks the site). Close to the market, you will see cars parked alongside the road. It is best, though, to park in the lot next to the market itself. Getting here by public transit could be difficult; if you are contemplating trying it, contact Lyon's tourist office to find out available routes.

IN MANY WAYS, LYON FEELS LIKE A SMALLER, MORE MANAGEABLE VERSION OF PARIS. ITS BROAD AVENUES LINED WITH LONG BLOCKS OF ORNATE GRAY-STONED buildings are very reminiscent of Paris, as are its grand public edifices like the Hôtel de Ville and the Musée des Beaux Arts. Even the riverside vistas, along the Rhône in particular, bring to mind the Seine in the early morning. Yet there is a more luminous, pale quality to the light here which makes you soon realize that you are actually about 500 kilometers south of Paris, just above the northern fringes of Provence.

Once in the center (well away from the unsightly autoroutes which encircle the city), who can resist this place? Even if underwhelmed by its *vieille ville* (I confess that, apart from the wonderful *traboules*—the little passageways once used by silk workers to transport their wares—I found this part of town disappointing), Lyon is a very impressive city. Its growth and success owes much to the silk business, a primary activity from the sixteenth to twentieth centuries, when the chemical, metal and high-tech sectors took over, along with banking. Today, this feels like a very cosmo-politan and prosperous place.

The heart of Lyon is Presqu'île—the area between the Saône and Rhône rivers. This cultural and business center boasts wonderful pedestrian shopping streets and large squares (the huge place Bellecour and the more modest place Carnot). It exudes a feeling of grandeur in both its setting and its architecture, shown to its best advan-tage at night, by the use of dramatic lighting. And the more residential areas to the east of the Rhône (where you will find the train station, as well as Lyon's exceptional food market) are peaceful and charming.

Lyon is widely considered the culinary heart of France, both in terms of the variety and quality of its produce and its many renowned restaurants (famous for both *nouvelle cuisine* and more hearty regional fare). A great attraction are the Lyonnais *bouchons*—small, lively and accessible restaurants that serve up traditional Lyonnais fare in casual and friendly surroundings. After a couple of days walking, shopping and eating here, you will surely conclude that Lyon is a great place to spend time.

THE MARKET

The one thing the center of Lyon lacks is a regular flea market. To find that, you do not, however, have to travel far—just to the huge Sunday morning market in Villeurbanne, a few kilometers to the northeast of the city center. It is well worth the visit. The Villeurbanne market is one of the largest, and most interesting, in France. There are about 400 vendors here, including those who have permanent booths in a building on site. Some vendors are located under a metal roof outside, while the majority set up impromptu tables in long rows in the giant open air area next door, in front of the vans which have transported them and their wares from the surrounding region. Several of the vendors forego tables altogether, simply piling their merchandise onto blankets on the ground.

The setting is basic and not what you would call aesthetically pleasing (though there is a pleasant enough bike path alongside the canal, used by some to reach the market). But, unpolished though it is, I love the atmosphere here. In any event, you come to the Villeurbanne flea market for the *chine*, not the scenery. There is just about everything here, with a fair emphasis on the rustic, as opposed to the decorative, although you will see plenty of both. From the license plates on the vans, it is clear that vendors come from a large radius around Lyon, including Burgundy, Provence and the Alps, which helps explain the presence of so many rustic and functional everyday items from decades past. You will see agricultural collectibles, milk jugs, cow bells, oil lamps, colorful old soda bottles, fireplace bellows, garden accessories, coffee mills, books, glassware, toys, *boules* and Provençal and Savoyard ceramics and linens. There is also a surprising amount of furniture here—large primitive armoires and wooden chests as well as more formal pieces. (Recently, I saw a set of exceptionally ugly, but amazing, dining chairs made with antlers.)

While this is a very eclectic market, drawing from many regions (it is, after all, located at a crossroads of France), you will also spot collectibles particularly associated with Lyon and its environs—for instance, wooden blocks with elaborate patterns and old wooden spindles (used in the textile industry), chocolate molds, wine tasters and wine-making items.

This is a very busy flea market, as the many cars lined up along the road and in the crowded parking lot attest. People come to do serious buying here, both from Lyon and elsewhere in France, as well as from abroad. On a recent visit, I heard a few people with American accents, somewhat surprising in the middle of winter. Prices are moderate, not low, but vendors are quite prepared to bargain and are interested in making a sale, particularly as the morning advances. This is one market where coming early is a good idea, if you have hopes of finding something special.

OTHER THINGS TO DO

The flea market boasts a number of small cafés interspersed among the stalls, selling not just coffee and snacks, but also hearty *plats du jour*. A few vendors have also set up grills, serving up sausages in baguettes. Especially wonderful is La Grande Boulangerie du Canal, a bakery/café, decorated with flea market finds, in the middle of the market, serving delicious quiches, pizzas and brownies, as well as breads, croissants and *pains au chocolat*. (It is no accident, surely, that such good fare can be found even here.)

Once you have finished at the market, you will want to head back to the city center. If you are not particularly drawn to high-end, high-priced dining, and relish some hearty Lyonnais fare—*saucisses*, *boudin* (blood sausage), *andouillette* (tripe sausage), *quenelles* (dumplings usually made with fish, and bathed in sauce), *cervelle de canut* ("*fromage frais*" mixed with various herbs), or *salade Lyonnaise*, served with *lardons* and poached egg—try one of Lyon's many *bouchons*, the homey and unpretentious eateries that abound in the city. (The name likely comes from the verb *bouchonner*, meaning to "rub down." The story is that these were spots where horses could be rubbed down with straw and their riders could obtain sustenance.)

A great choice for a *bouchon* meal is La Meunière (11, rue Neuve, tel. 04-78-28-62-91), just off the rue de la République, one of Lyon's best shopping streets. In the evenings, this small place is jammed with customers sitting together at long tables, sharing cheese, bread, big bowls of lentils and conversation. When we asked our fellow diners here to define the *bouchon*, they replied that it is an especially convivial place to eat. There is certainly a lot of friendly bantering between the patrons and customers, and among the customers themselves, in this place. After passing the communal bread basket to our neighbors, we were soon sharing our dishes and launching into a wide-ranging conversation which finally ended as the restaurant emptied.

If you are looking for a fun and unusually relaxed café, try Café 203, named after the Peugeot of the same model number (9, rue de Garet). At the other end of the spectrum, for a truly grand and luxurious café experience, head to the place Francisque Régaud, where you will find the well-over-a-century-old Grand Café des Négotiants, with its plush, opulent décor and elaborate chandeliers.

You cannot leave Lyon without spending some time at its wonderful food market, Les Halles de Lyon (102, cours Lafayette, in Part Dieu not far from the train station), which dates back to 1859. Don't be turned off by its nondescript, modern building. What is inside will amaze you if the architecture doesn't. The choice of cheeses (runny, ripe Saint-Marcellins, a specialty here), sausages, fish, *quenelles*, oysters, pastries, bread and produce is almost too overwhelming. You can even sit down and try some oysters or typical Lyonnais fare at one of the small eateries set up in the market itself. The market's website describes this food market as "*une institution chère à chaque Lyonnais*" (an institution dear to each Lyonnais). If it isn't, it should be.

And, since you are in the neighborhood, you must also pay a visit to the shrine to chocolate, Bernachon (42, cours Franklin Roosevelt, tel. 04-78-24-37-98), considered one of the best chocolate makers in the world. Its signature *palet d'or*, with little flecks of gold in it, is a taste sensation. And for a very good, and remarkably inexpensive lunch nearby, in comfortable surroundings, try Le Restaurant d'Olivier (125, rue de Sèze, tel. 04-78-24-41-26).

OTHER NEARBY MARKETS

South of Lyon, but north of Vienne, the town of Givors has a good-sized flea market on the third Saturday morning of the month, in the parking lot of the Jacques Anquetil stadium (along the R.N. 86).

STRASBOURG
Wednesday and Saturday

Number of Vendors: 25 on Wednesday, up to 40 on Saturday
Price-Quality: ⚜ ⚜ – ⚜ ⚜ ⚜
Scenic Value: ⚜ ⚜ – ⚜ ⚜ ⚜ • Amenities Nearby: ⚜ ⚜ ⚜ – ⚜ ⚜ ⚜ ⚜

FEATURED ITEMS

Alsatian ceramics, Lorraine dishware, beer steins, clocks, glassware, linens, toys, furniture, rustic items generally

MARKET DETAILS

Strasbourg has a small flea market twice a week—on Wednesdays and Saturdays, with several more vendors on Saturday than on Wednesday (and more during the summer than the winter). While the hours are listed as all day, several vendors begin to pack up just after noon, so it is strongly advised to come in the morning. The market takes place on the rue du Vieil Hôpital and the adjacent place de la Grande Boucherie, in the center of town, not far from the cathedral. If arriving by train, the market is about a 15-minute walk from the station. From the place de la Gare, take the rue du Maire Kuss, cross the Ill River, and then continue east on the rue du 22 Novembre. Turn right on the rue des Francs-Bourgeois and then left on the rue

des Serruriers, which runs into the place Gutenberg. On the other side of the square, take the rue Mercière; the first street on the right is the rue du Vieil Hôpital, the site of the market. (You can also take a tram from the station, which will drop you nearby.)

THOUGH LOCATED ON THE NORTHEAST EDGE OF FRANCE, FAR FROM OTHER MAJOR URBAN CENTERS, STRASBOURG HAS THE FEEL OF AN IMPORTANT French city. It has a distinguished history; first settled by the Romans 2,000 years ago, it was a prosperous trading center during the Middle Ages. Another reason for its stature, of course, is its strategic location—on the Rhine River, bordering Germany. Today Strasbourg plays a pivotal role in the great European project. This is, after all, the home of the European Parliament, as well as the Council of Europe and the European Court of Human Rights. And, despite its significant distance from Paris—about 500 kilometers—you can get here in under two and a half hours, thanks to France's high-speed train, the TGV.

Strasbourg has a dual identity—that of regional center of Alsatian culture, on the one hand, and cosmopolitan, international player, on the other. Its own past reflects that duality. Strasbourg was united with France until the latter part of the seventeenth century, and between 1871 and the end of World War I, and again during World War II, it, like much of Alsace and Lorraine, was annexed by Germany. The city's Alsatian heritage is reflected not just in its architecture—for example, in the colorful half-timbered buildings lining the narrow streets of Petite France—but also in its hearty Alsatian cuisine and its language. Many residents speak German, as well as French, but they also still speak Alsatian (based on a German dialect, with a number of other influences mixed in).

THE MARKET

Strasbourg's twice weekly flea market is surprisingly small, given the stature of the city. On Wednesdays and Saturdays, around 25 to 40 vendors (several more on Saturday than Wednesday) set up on the rue du Vieil Hôpital and the adjoining place de la Grande Boucherie, in the center of town. There are also more vendors here during the busy summer months than in the much quieter, and sometimes quite chilly, winter. Though located in the city's historic heart, this is not the most picturesque setting; however, given the competition, that is a high standard indeed, and the location is pleasant and quiet.

Some of the vendors set up at tables which appealingly showcase their wares, while others simply set out boxes on the ground for prospective buyers to rifle through; the quality of the goods—and the prices—vary accordingly. Despite the small number of merchants, there is a wide variety in the wares here. A major focus is on collectibles from Alsace and neighboring Lorraine. Alsatian ceramics, in particular, are popular, in old jugs and bowls bearing the signature tones of rust, straw, pale green and blue with images of small flowers or geometric patterns. (Many hail from the town of Soufflenheim, nearby.) You will also see stoneware jugs—in gray with blue blotches—from Betschdorf, further north, as well as rust-colored ceramic baking molds, for making the signature Alsatian *kugelhopf* cake. (You may also spot molds shaped like lambs and fish, used for Easter cakes.) The popular Alsatian symbol of the stork can be found on faïence from Lunéville (in Lorraine), while folk images decorate dishware from Sarreguemines (also in Lorraine). And you are also likely to see linens embroidered in red with Alsatian folk designs.

Of course, this market also has collectibles from other parts of France, and neighboring Germany—silver, copperware, glassware, clocks and toys, as well as rustic tools and other items. Vendors are friendly—one declared recently, upon learning that I was from North America, that "*le monde est ma cour de récréation*" ("The world is my playground"), and he seemed to mean it. Vendors are also keen to make a sale, and so are willing to bargain. I heard one ask a young man inquiring about the price of something, "*Quels sont vos moyens?*" (basically, "What can you afford to pay?"). Despite this market's small size, I have found some nice things here at reasonable prices, and while I would not suggest a detour to see it, I would recommend checking the market out for a few minutes if you are in town on these days.

OTHER THINGS TO DO

You must try some Alsatian cuisine when you are here, and a very good restaurant for that—which also happens to be right in the midst of the flea market—is Zuem Strissel (5 place de la Grande Boucherie, tel. 03-88-32-14-73). This atmospheric spot, which dates back to the sixteenth century, is popular with tourists and locals alike. (The waiter first addressed me in what I took to be German, and when I replied that we did not speak German, he answered, somewhat indignantly, that he had actually been speaking Alsatian.) The restaurant is noted for its *choucroute* (great, washed down with some Riesling) and for its other regional fare—*tarte flambée*, a kind of Alsatian pizza, and all sorts of pork dishes.

For a comfortable, old-fashioned *salon de thé*, decorated with Alsatian ceramics and frequented by locals, try Winter (25, rue du 22 Novembre). To get real insight into some of the everyday collectibles of this region, visit the Musée Alsatien (23, quai Saint-Nicolas, tel. 03-88-52-50-01). Afterwards (though I generally avoid such

touristy activities), I highly recommend a boat tour of the city, which leaves from just below the cathedral. It not only takes you through Petite France, but also goes as far as the city's European institutions, giving you a great waterside perspective of Strasbourg's residential areas en route.

OTHER NEARBY MARKETS

There are very few regular flea markets in the vicinity, although Colmar to the south has a small all-day Friday market, in the place des Dominicains.

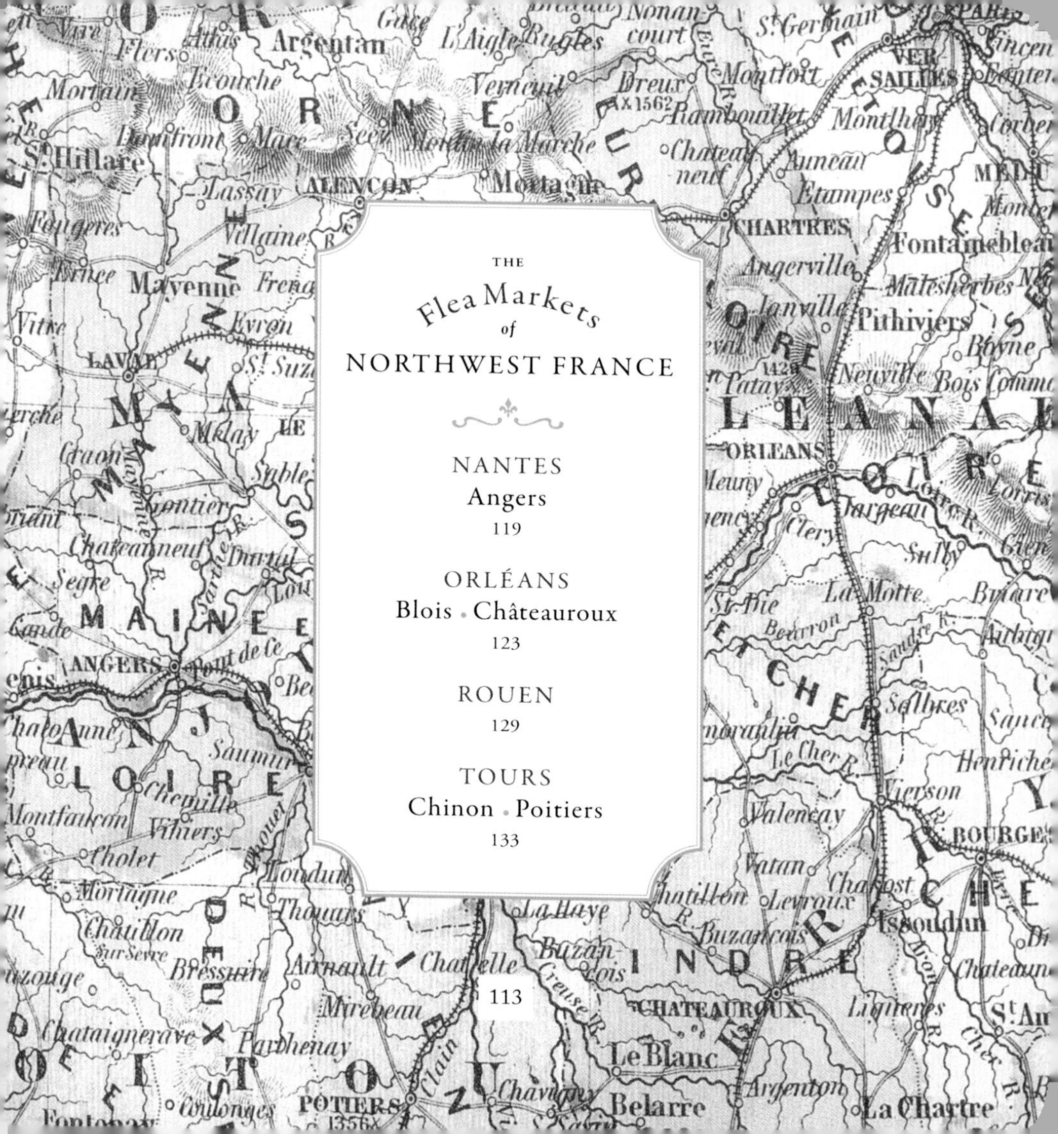

THE

Flea Markets of NORTHWEST FRANCE

ABOUT THE REGION

THE NORTHWEST CORNER OF FRANCE EMBRACES A NUMBER OF REGIONS, INCLUDING NORMANDY AND BRITTANY, WITH THEIR STRONG MARITIME character, and the pastoral Loire valley. These three areas are hugely popular tourist destinations, among both the French and foreigners. They are also conveniently accessed from Paris. (By high speed train you can be in Tours in just over an hour, and in Nantes in two, for example.)

These are wonderful places to visit—Brittany with its Celtic roots, charming coastal towns, *galettes* and great seafood and Normandy with its long beaches, Calvados, fresh dairy products and its important sites—the D-day beaches, the Bayeux tapestry and Mont Saint-Michel, to name just a few. The Loire offers its gentle countryside, harmonious *châteaux*, and great wine and cuisine (including impeccably fresh produce, game, fish and goat cheese). You could easily spend several weeks touring this part of France without running out of things to see.

The countryside and the little towns and villages here are its biggest attractions, but the larger urban areas also have their charms. Nantes, on the edge of Brittany, offers its impressive Château des Ducs de Bretagne and a pleasing city center. Rouen, despite extensive bombardments during World War ll, boasts its intricately carved cathedral (so immortalized by Monet) and pristine *vieille ville* of colorful half-timbered buildings. Tours also has a lively, medieval center, and Orléans (perhaps the most transformed in recent years) showcases its graceful arcaded streets.

ABOUT THE MARKETS

This corner of France is not as well endowed with flea markets as others, but the ones it does have are impressive, both in size and quality of the wares. The markets are mostly concentrated in the larger towns and cities, within easy access of the train station. The monthly flea market in Tours is one of the most significant in France, with around 140 vendors. The weekly markets in Nantes and Orléans are also substantial (at about 100 vendors), while Rouen has smaller, but more frequent, ones. There are also a number of other smaller flea markets—for example, in Angers and Rennes—which take place on a weekly basis.

I really like the range of these markets, in both kinds of collectibles and prices. They fall within that nice middle ground; neither too low-end nor too high-brow (Tours being perhaps the most high-end). You will not see a lot of secondhand goods—like clothing and toys—piled on the ground, although they are not completely absent. On the other hand, things have not been so carefully filtered and polished that the chance of making a good find at a good price is negated. There is also a very wide variety in the range of collectibles—from rustic to decorative—as well as in prices.

As is true generally in France, the rustic items here reflect the region's traditional economic base—farming, fishing and wine-making. You will see large glass domes (called *cloches*), used in the Loire to cover plants, fishing gear of all kinds and implements for making wine (in the Loire) and cider (in Normandy). There are also lots of other regional collectibles to look out for—porcelain from Limoges, faïence from Gien and from Normandy, the highly popular folkloric ceramics from Quimper, copper pots from Normandy, biscuit tins from Nantes and baskets and tapestries from the area around Tours. You will also see lace and lacemaking tools, marine and nautical items, World War II memorabilia, butter molds, cider jugs and Breton dolls.

WHEN TO GO ✤ HOW TO TRAVEL

This region can be quite cold and damp in the winter, so if at all possible try to come during the warmer months of the year. The flea markets will also be a lot busier then. August can be almost too crowded, notably in Brittany, a favored destination of the French who generally take their holidays then.

The great thing about some of these markets—the ones in Tours, Orléans and Rouen, especially—is that they can be visited (along with the city itself) in a day trip from Paris, given their quick access by train. So, if you want to see a number of flea markets, and like the idea of not having to lug your baggage around, consider booking an apartment for a week or two in Paris, and traveling out to the markets from there. On the other hand, if seeing the markets is just part of your plan for acquainting yourself with the region, rent a car. Driving here is pleasant, and you can easily avoid traveling on the autoroute, if you wish.

NANTES
Saturday morning

Number of Vendors: 100 · Price-Quality: ⚜ ⚜ – ⚜ ⚜ ⚜

Scenic Value: ⚜ ⚜ · Amenities Nearby: ⚜ ⚜ – ⚜ ⚜ ⚜

FEATURED ITEMS

Quimper ceramics, nautical items, kitchenware, tins, paintings,
tools, linens, African collectibles, books

MARKET DETAILS

The Nantes flea market takes place on Saturday mornings in the place Viarme, in the northwestern part of town close to the center. If arriving by train, take Tram 1 west, to the Commerce stop, and then Tram 3 north, to the Viarme-Talensac stop. The market is right here, on both sides of the tram line.

NANTES IS A SIGNIFICANT CITY, WITH OVER A QUARTER MILLION INHABITANTS. WHILE IT MAY NOT BE A BIG TOURIST DESTINATION IN ITS OWN right, its nineteenth-century center is graceful and pleasing, with store-lined pedestrian streets leading into spacious squares. Though located along the Loire River, Nantes was once an important center of Brittany, and its former capital. The Château des Ducs de Bretagne, built in the fifteenth century and site of the signing of the Edict of Nantes in 1598, attests to that historical relation-ship.

During the eighteenth century, this was a prosperous city indeed, thanks to ship-building and trade with the colonies and, sadly, the slave trade. That prosperity is demonstrated by the nineteenth century center, with its ornate, covered Passage de Pommeraye (an early version of the shopping mall), decorated with statues, elabo-rate gas lamps and a fine glass ceiling.

THE MARKET

Nantes has a significant and well-established flea market, dating back several decades. It takes place on Saturday mornings in the place Viarme. The setting is not picturesque, but it is certainly convenient, as it is located right at the Viarme-Talensac tramway stop. About 100 vendors arrange their wares here, in long rows on both sides of the line.

This is a promising market for those hoping to uncover something interesting at a good price. Several of the vendors offer a very eclectic mix of collectibles, sometimes piled in boxes for browsers to sort through. You can find Quimper pieces in among jumbles of dishware, although finer pieces are likely to be more attractively dis-played—and hence more expensive—on tables or arranged on blankets.

This is a good market for those looking for rustic items—tools, agricultural im-plements, hardware and carved wooden objects. You will also see everyday kitchen collectibles of all sorts, from different parts of France. More decorative pieces can also be found—paintings, vases, 60s collectibles, porcelain and African statues—vying for space with the more functional fare. Books and postcards are popular, as well.

Bargaining is brisk and serious, as this is a market for people who come to buy, rather than simply to browse. If you are a collector, I would certainly try to fit the Nantes flea market into your itinerary for a tour of either the Loire or Brittany.

OTHER THINGS TO DO

After visiting the market, be sure to check out what is by far the most beautiful café/*brasserie* that I have seen in France—the late-nineteenth-century La Cigale, in the place Graslin (4, tel. 02-51-84-94-94) . With its elaborately painted ceilings, beveled mirrors, whimsical moldings and colorful, folkloric tiles of dancing *cigales* (cicadas), this is a magical place. La Cigale also serves a fine coffee and a reasonably priced lunch menu. Sitting here, gazing out across the square at the imposing Grand Théâtre, is hard to beat.

OTHER NEARBY MARKETS

The town of Angers, about 100 kilometers northeast of Nantes, also has a Saturday morning flea market, in the place Imbach. This market, more moderate in size, has around 50 to 60 vendors.

ORLÉANS
Saturday morning

Number of Vendors: 100 to 120 · Price-Quality: ⚜ ⚜ – ⚜ ⚜ ⚜
Scenic Value: ⚜ ⚜ · Amenities Nearby: ⚜ ⚜ – ⚜ ⚜ ⚜

FEATURED ITEMS

garden accessories, tools, fishing gear, kitchenware, ceramics,
Gien and Limoges dishes, linens, dolls, books, pewter

MARKET DETAILS

The Orléans flea market takes place on Saturday morning on the boulevard Alexandre Martin on the northeast edge of the center of town. If arriving by train, it is about a five-minute walk from the station. Go south on the avenue de Paris, and then turn left on the boulevard de Verdun, which becomes the boulevard A. Martin just east of the place Albert 1er, where the market begins. If arriving by car, the market is located a couple of blocks north of the central cathedral Sainte-Croix, and runs southeast off the place Gambetta. Look for meter parking along the street near the market.

OFF THE RADAR OF MOST TOURIST ITINERARIES, ORLÉANS OFFERS VISITORS A STEP-
PING-OFF POINT TO THE LOIRE REGION ITSELF, THOUGH ITS GRAND
architecture and lovely arcade-lined squares are not typical of that part of
France. Rather, Orléans seems more oriented toward Paris, about 130 kilometers away,
and the city is increasingly a commuter town for people working there, who want
space, affordable housing and a pleasant lifestyle. I noticed a big change in this city of
around 100,000 inhabitants when I came here recently after many years' absence.
Orléans seems to have been given a substantial facelift. The luminous pale stone on
the buildings, sidewalks and arcades has received a major scrubbing, and the narrow
pedestrian streets lined with attractive cafés and restaurants are well-maintained and
lively. And, for a bit of nature, there is a paved pedestrian and bicycle path alongside
the Loire, where you can watch people fishing in the early morning mist.

Orléans has a long history, its most notable moment being its liberation from the
English in 1429 (during the Hundred Years' War), with the help of the young Joan of
Arc. Joan is immortalized here, most noticeably in the large statue of her on horse-
back in the majestic place du Martroi. It is said that she celebrated the victory in the
cathedral Sainte-Croix, the imposing edifice which dominates the center of town.
(Joan of Arc was, of course, later imprisoned and executed in Rouen, as a heretic.)

THE MARKET

The Orléans flea market is well established and substantial. Between 100 and 120
vendors set up their wares on Saturday morning, in the large parking lot alongside
the boulevard A. Martin on the edge of the center.

The market has that nice balance—neither too down-home nor too high-end—and caters to both collectors of rustic, everyday collectibles and those interested in more decorative items. It will also appeal to both those who enjoy foraging to unearth a treasure and those who prefer collectibles that are clean and well-presented. Prices are moderate, neither low nor high, and vendors—a mix of professionals and ordinary people apparently trying to dispense with their belongings—are willing to bargain.

Many of the collectibles here are a reflection of the surrounding *terroir*. You will see many agricultural and gardening items—the (highly coveted) large glass domes (called *cloches de maraîcher*) once used to protect young plants and the accessories and implements used for making wine in this region. You will also come across all sorts of fishing gear, used for snaring trout and other fish from the Loire and the smaller rivers around it.

Collectors of quotidian kitchen collectibles—dishes, glassware, copper pots, enamel ware, *café au lait* bowls, utensils—will also enjoy foraging here. In addition to rustic brown-speckled regional ceramics, you will see more decorative dishware from nearby Gien and Limoges, as well as from other regions of France, including Brittany and Alsace. I noticed a fair number of *barbotine* dishes here, including a few copies of a plate with the image of Joan of Arc herself. Linens, both more rustic and fine, are popular, offered at competitive prices. (I bought, for seven euros, a set of six finely woven *torchons* [dish towels] from the Pays Basque, a region renowned for its high-quality linens. I also bought an old jadite glass yogurt container, for two euros.) You will also find books, paintings, some rustic furniture and dolls.

OTHER THINGS TO DO

After visiting the market, head for lunch (or dinner) to the pedestrian rue de Bourgogne. One popular restaurant worth trying is La Petite Marmite (number 178, tel. 02-38-54-23-83). The food, while not exceptional, is nicely prepared, the service attentive and the surroundings comfortable—with wooden beams, and prints and decorative plates on the walls. For a really good *café au lait* (actually very hard to find in France, where fresh milk is often not used) and a flaky quiche Lorraine or a pastry, try Les Musardises, a colorful, somewhat old-fashioned *salon de thé* (38, rue de la République, the main shopping street close to both the train station and the flea market).

OTHER NEARBY MARKETS

Blois, further southwest along the Loire between Orléans and Tours, has a moderate-sized flea market on the second Sunday of the month, all day, in the Mail Saint-Jean. And, about 100 kilometers south of Orléans, Châteauroux has a very large market, on the first Sunday of the month, except August and September (all day in October, morning only November to July) along the avenue des Marins.

ROUEN
Thursday morning

Number of Vendors: 50 · Price-Quality: ✿✿
Scenic Value: ✿–✿✿ · Amenities Nearby: ✿✿

FEATURED ITEMS

kitchenware, glassware, postcards, ceramics, linens, books, rustic items

MARKET DETAILS

Rouen has a flea market on Thursday mornings, in the place des Emmurées, in the southern part of Rouen (the Rive Gauche), south of the Seine. From the train station, take the subway south, exiting at the Joffre-Mutualité stop. The market is just to the southeast of the exit; follow the cours Clemenceau east, then turn right on the rue François Arago, which leads into the place des Emmurées.

JUST OVER AN HOUR FROM PARIS BY TRAIN, ROUEN IS WELL WORTH A VISIT. IT IS A PLACE WHERE HISTORY HAS PLAYED A DRAMATIC ROLE. FIRST occupied by the Gauls and the Romans, over a thousand years ago it became the capital of Normandy. Control over Rouen was bitterly disputed by the French and the English during the Hundred Years' War, and after enduring a lengthy siege, the city fell for three decades of the fifteenth century to the English. This was during the time of Joan of Arc, who was tried and executed here for witchcraft and heresy.

Though Rouen suffered significant damage from Allied bombardments during the Second World War, its historic center remains largely intact. While not large, it is packed with impressive attractions. In addition to the colorful, half-timbered buildings, its pedestrian rue du Gros-Horloge is overseen by the opulent Gros Horloge (moved here during the sixteenth century). The most famous site, though, is the ornate Cathédrale de Notre Dame nearby, immortalized in so many paintings by Monet. An eerie, but remarkable, spot is the Aître Saint-Maclou, a burial site for victims of the plague during the Middle Ages—the woodwork on the buildings lining the square is decorated with carvings of skeletons and burial tools.

Of course, there are all the reminders of Joan of Arc—the tower where she was tried and imprisoned, the cross in the place du Vieux Marché where she was burned at the stake, and the modern Église Jeanne d'Arc, its undulating roof evoking either flames or a boat, depending on your perspective.

THE MARKET

Across the river from the center of Rouen, in an area removed from the splendors of its medieval past, is the place des Emmurées market. It takes place in the open ground floor of a parking lot, hardly an auspicious location. And yet the neighborhood—with its many food stores, butcher shops and bakeries—is not unpleasant. Starting very early Thursday morning, about 50 to 60 vendors arrive and set up tables here, or simply arrange their wares on the ground. Dealers and curious collectors arrive early as well, armed with flashlights to check out the goods as they are being unpacked. By noon, most of the vendors have at least begun the process of packing up again.

This is a market for fans of everyday and rustic collectibles, rather than those looking for fine decorative items in pristine condition. There is a wide range in the quality and variety of the goods—the last time I was here, I spotted a stuffed wild boar head, an old porcelain bedpan, some very dusty bottles of wine and sinister-looking old glass pharmacy bottles. You will see ceramics (faïence from the region, as well as Quimper, Alsatian ceramics and porcelain), kitchenware, linens, books, postcards, copper pots, vases, and more. Prices are quite reasonable, and bargaining is certainly practiced. While this is not a market I would recommend to those wishing to take away a romantic image of Rouen and its past—or general tourists, for that matter—it is worth a brief visit for collectors of everyday items looking for a bit of a bargain. For that, come early if you can.

OTHER THINGS TO DO

For a light lunch, in a friendly, pleasant atmosphere, try Le Saint Romain, a *crêperie* and *saladerie* right in the center of the old town (52, rue Saint-Romain, tel. 02-35-88-90-36). There is also a charming—albeit very flowery—*salon de thé* nearby, called Dame Cakes (70, rue Saint-Romain, tel. 02-35-07-49-31).

As Rouen has historically been a center of decorative faïence dishes, check out some of the *ateliers* in town where this tradition is being perpetuated. One that I found impressive, with helpful service, is Faïences Saint Romain, also on Saint-Romain, at number 56 (tel., 02-35-07-12-30).

OTHER NEARBY MARKETS

Rouen has another flea market, as part of its general food market, on Friday, Saturday and Sunday mornings, in the place Saint-Marc in the center of town. (Some of the place des Emmurées dealers also sell here.) If possible, try to come Sunday, when the flea market (with up to 50 vendors) is larger than on the other two days. The setting—a large square lined with imposing red brick buildings—will appeal to general tourists as well as collectors.

TOURS
First Sunday
of the month

Number of Vendors: 140 · Price-Quality: ❧❧–❧❧❧
Scenic Value: ❧❧–❧❧❧ · Amenities Nearby: ❧❧❧

FEATURED ITEMS

porcelain and ceramics (from Gien, Limoges and elsewhere),
silver, glassware, fine linens and lace, books, paintings,
tapestries, jardinizres, coffee mills, furniture

MARKET DETAILS

Tours has a large flea market that takes place on the fourth Sunday of the month, all day, along the boulevard Béranger in the center of town. If arriving by train, the market is about a five-minute walk from the central station (as distinct from the Saint-Pierre des Corps station, where the TGV trains depart). Upon exiting, head north through the place du Général Leclerc to the boulevard Heurteloup, then turn left. After the place Jean Jaurès it becomes the boulevard Béranger, the site of the market. If arriving by car, you should be able to find parking on nearby streets.

OURS IS THE URBAN CENTER OF THE LOIRE REGION, THE POINT FROM WHICH MANY VISITORS COMMENCE THEIR TOUR OF THE *CHÂTEAUX*. IT HAS THE distinct advantage of being very accessible to Paris; it is only around an hour on the TGV, even though it is over 230 kilometers away. Increasingly, people commute from here to Paris to work, helping make this city of about 130,000 people a lively and prosperous-looking place. There is also a large student population in Tours, contributing to its energetic feel.

The architecture of the city combines both medieval and modern styles, the unfortunate result of the major bombing Tours endured during World War II. Its *vieille ville*, however, is quite intact, and almost too picturesque to be true. Half-timbered, centuries-old brick buildings, some with wonderfully carved dark wooden beams, line the place Plumereau, whose cafés are packed with people, especially on a sunny day. And on Saturday afternoons the nearby rue Nationale is busy with shoppers. Tours also has some wide boulevards, reminiscent of Paris, giving parts of the city a bourgeois, almost stolid look.

THE MARKET

The flea market along the boulevard Béranger, which takes place on the fourth Sunday of the month, is one of the best in France, in size, quality and range of goods. Around 140 vendors set up shop here in two long rows in the middle of the boulevard, a pleasant space edged by plane trees. Most vendors here deal in particular collectibles, and the quality of their wares is generally high. Prices follow accordingly, but this is still a market where a good find can be had at a reasonable price.

There is a very wide variety in the things for sale at this market. Unlike the market of nearby Orléans, however, the emphasis is more on finer, decorative items, as opposed to rustic, everyday collectibles (although, happily, they are not entirely absent). Porcelain and ceramics are a big feature—from nearby Gien and Limoges, but also from elsewhere in France. *Barbotine* plates, *jardinières,* and fine china vie with Quimper dishes and rustic jugs from both the Loire and Alsace. Also popular are fine linens, lace and tapestries, reminiscent of the industries which supplied the *châteaux* and finer homes of yesteryear. Crystal, glassware and silver are also to be found, along with lots of books and paintings.

Rustic items—tools, agricultural implements and wooden objects (boxes, old wooden shoes, etc.)—are clean and well-polished, which is reflected in the price. And while the emphasis is on better-quality collectibles, this is an eclectic market where surprise often awaits the passersby. The last time I came, I saw leather pouches used to make lace, a German saddle from World War II and a stuffed fox.

I would rank this as a must-see market in this region (and France generally). The atmosphere is upbeat and cheerful, with lots of people strolling along, particularly during the warmer months. Trucks tucked in among vendors' tables offer *crêpes* and coffee, sandwiches and pastries. (One woman gave us samples for free, when we enquired about her pastries.) And, like the market in Orléans, this is one you can easily visit on a day trip from Paris, if you don't have more time than that to spend here.

OTHER THINGS TO DO

One of my favorite French dining experiences in a long while was a recent dinner here in a tiny place specializing in Touraine cuisine. The restaurant, tucked away in one of Tours's narrow streets, was highly recommended by a woman I met outside the train station. Le Petit Patrimoine (58, rue Colbert, tel. 02-47-66-05-81), as the cover of its menu so aptly puts it, sees its mission as offering "*un hommage à la Touraine et à ses produits du terroir*" (homage to the Tours region and its products of the land). It is a real gem, presided over by an energetic young man, whose enthusiasm about his region and its cuisine is infectious. The food is not only delicious and beautifully presented, it is also extremely well-priced. Goat cheese from the region, local fish and a flaky *tourte* with *rillons* (crisp pork belly) were some of the items on the menu when we were there. Make a reservation though, since seating is very limited and this restaurant is popular.

If you just want to grab a quick snack on the run, be sure to check out Briocherie Lelong (13, place Général-Leclerc) near the train station. Around 3 p.m. people line up outside this place, which has been run by the Lelong family for a century, to purchase a fresh, warm brioche.

OTHER NEARBY MARKETS

A modest-size flea market also takes place in Tours on Wednesdays and Saturdays (until just after midday) in the place de la Victoire, on the edge of the *vieille ville*. There is also a small *brocante* market on the first and third Friday of the month on the rue de Bordeaux.

To the east, the town of Blois has a medium-sized market on the second Sunday of the month, while Angers to the west has a pleasant flea market on Saturday mornings, in the place Imbach. Not far southwest of Tours, Chinon has an all-day flea market on the third Sunday of the month, in the place Tiverton.

If you are venturing southeast from Tours, the workaday town of Châteauroux has

a very large, down-home flea market on the first Sunday of the month from October to July (morning only November to July, all day in October). To the southwest, in Poitiers, there is an interesting moderate-sized market on Fridays, all day (and on the fourth Sunday of the month) in the place Charles de Gaulle, in front of the Notre-Dame-la-Grande church.

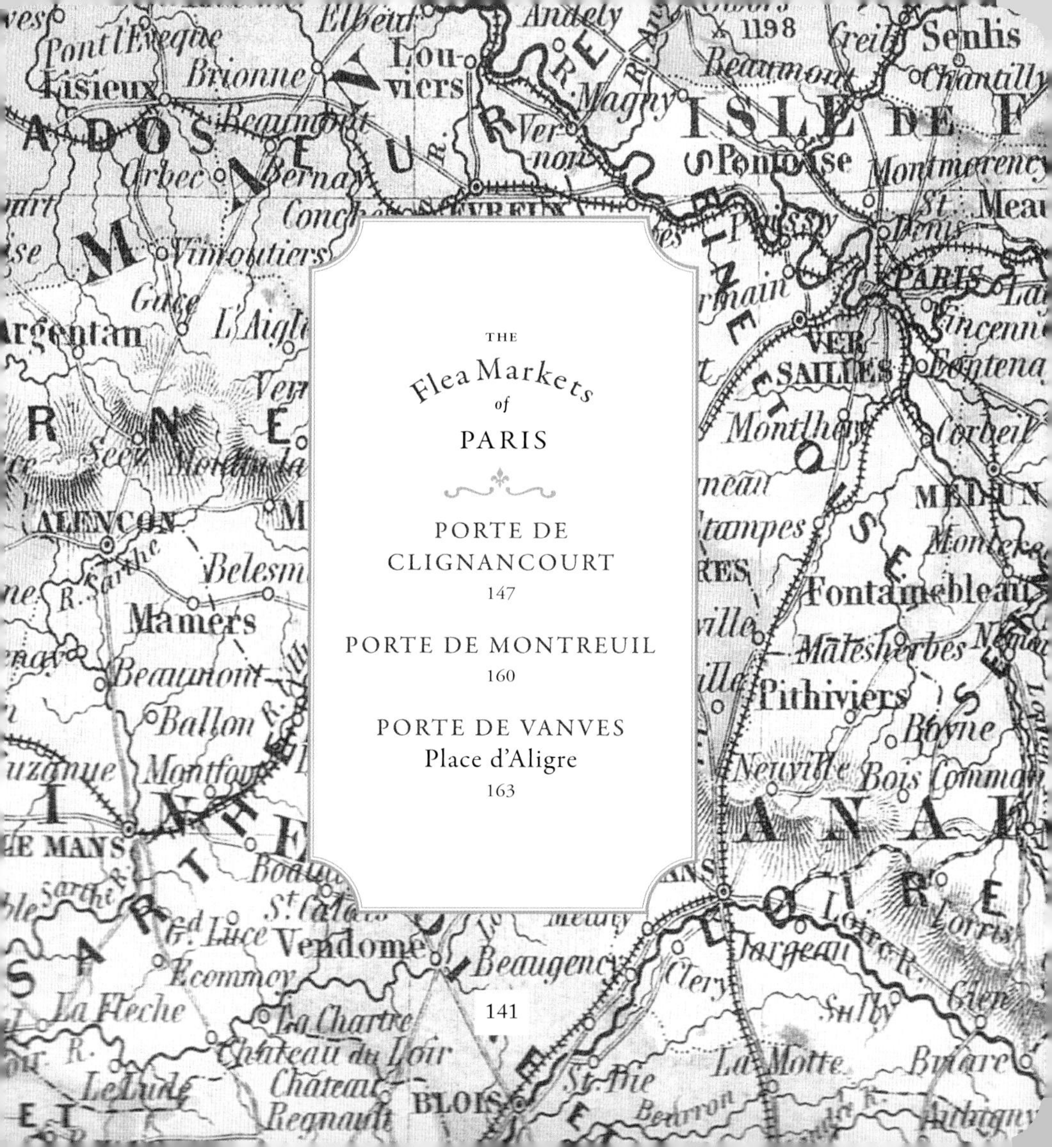

THE

Flea Markets

of

PARIS

❧⚜❧

PORTE DE
CLIGNANCOURT
147

PORTE DE MONTREUIL
160

PORTE DE VANVES
Place d'Aligre
163

GETTING ORIENTED

PARIS ITSELF, OF COURSE, NEEDS NO INTRODUCTION. HOWEVER, IT IS USEFUL TO HAVE SOME BACKGROUND INFORMATION ON THE FLEA MARKETS HERE, before checking them out. First-time visitors will otherwise be surprised by their out-of-the-way locations and less than aesthetic appearance. The three big markets featured in this chapter are all held at the edge of Paris, by the unsightly *boulevard périphérique*. (This is in stark contrast to most of the flea markets in France, which are held in the center of towns and cities, and often in stunning surroundings.) Even the Puces de Saint-Ouen—the queen of French flea markets to many—is located above the Porte de Clignancourt (the north end of the city), and is housed in a strange mix of ramshackle structures and modern buildings. The other two flea markets are similarly removed—the Porte de Montreuil market at the east end of Paris and the Porte de Vanves in the south—and similarly unaesthetic.

The flea markets of Paris are the product of their distinctive history, which dates back a few centuries to the rag and junk trade. At night, the streets would be scoured by individuals (sometimes referred to as *chiffoniers*, *biffins* and, more figuratively, *pêcheurs de lune*), scavenging for bits of scrap metal, rags and used objects of all kinds that could be sold for a profit.

In the nineteenth century, however, efforts were made to force these small-time "entrepreneurs" out of the city center. During the 1880s, in a measure to promote public hygiene, a city official named Poubelle (from which the French word for "garbage can" is derived) ordered that city garbage bins be sealed, dramatically cutting into the scavenger trade. Though the terms of the decree were later slightly moderated, this—as well as increasing city rents—had the effect of driving many of the scrap dealers out, to the periphery, especially to the north, in Saint-Ouen, just above the Porte de Clignancourt. Here, outside the city limits, they also avoided certain taxes.

By the mid-1880s, there was already a market of sorts operating at Saint-Ouen, where these scrap metal dealers sold their wares. They were soon joined by other used-goods dealers, who were busily scooping up bits of old furniture and bric-a-brac that the Parisian bourgeoisie, lured by the latest fashions, was increasingly keen to shed. By the mid-1890s, a flourishing flea market—a real *marché aux puces*—had developed. Indeed, a flea market fad swept the city. Parisians would head up here on weekends, and scour the secondhand goods and collectibles on offer in this outdoor space. And, not long into the twentieth century, they could get access to the market in short order, using the *métro* system.

The so-called permanent markets at Saint-Ouen evolved from these origins, beginning at the end of World War I, first with the Marché Vernaison and, a few years later, the Marché Malik. Others followed, with the last market, the Marché

Dauphine, opening in 1991. Ten years later, the Puces de Saint-Ouen were declared a protected heritage site.

The other two big flea markets in Paris had similar origins. The Porte de Vanves market, at the southern edge of the city, dates back to the early twentieth century (the exact date is hard to pin down), although its location changed a few times before it reached its present location in 1965. At the eastern edge, the Porte de Montreuil market, which also owes its origins to the rag and junk merchants, became particularly well established just after World War II.

Ironically, while the Porte de Clignancourt—with its permanent buildings and stalls—does not look like a typical flea market, it is, in fact, the natural, organic product of true *puces* origins in that very place. That said, though, of the three big Parisian markets today, it is the Porte de Vanves which represents for many the essence of the flea market experience—a place where, at stalls set up that morning and taken down later that day, some wonderful, unexpected treasures may be found.

GETTING AROUND

Very few visitors will have a car in Paris, which is fortunate since driving here is a challenge at best. Happily, all three of the markets profiled below are easily accessible via the city's reliable and efficient *métro* system, and located just a couple of minutes' walk from the station. I also strongly recommend taking public transit instead of a taxi, since a taxi ride to these markets from the center of town can be slow and expensive.

ABOUT THE COLLECTIBLES

The Parisian flea markets are particularly noteworthy for the wonderful array of collectibles they offer; you could run across just about anything here. If your travel plans do not afford you the opportunity to witness firsthand the extraordinary regional diversity of France, you can still find it in the flea markets of Paris. You will see ceramics and porcelain from all over—Provence, Brittany, the Pays Basque, the Côte d'Azur, the Loire, the Savoie and Alsace. You will also find fine linens from southwest France, *boules* and *santons* (ceramic folkloric figures) from Provence, copper pots from Normandy and cow bells from the Savoie. You will see wine-making collectibles from Burgundy, dolls from Brittany, clocks from Franche-Comté, butter molds from the Savoie and enamel plaques from Alsace.

But you will also find lots of collectibles from other parts of Europe and even North America, Asia and Africa, many no doubt brought by people who came from those places to settle here. I always marvel when I come across an old McCoy baking bowl or 50s Fire King glassware from the United States or Cornish ware from Britain. And, at the other end of the spectrum, you will see some collectibles linked to Paris itself—for example, posters, old maps, advertising items and vintage souvenirs.

Together, these markets also run the gamut in terms of range in price and quality—from the rock-bottom Porte de Montreuil to the stratospheric Porte de Clignancourt, with the Porte de Vanves in between. This, together with the huge variety in the things for sale, makes the Parisian flea markets particularly exciting.

PORTE DE
CLIGNANCOURT
(PUCES DE SAINT-OUEN)
Saturday, Sunday &
Monday

Number of Vendors: 2000 to 3000 (fewer on Monday)

Price - Quality: ⚜ ⚜ ⚜ – ⚜ ⚜ ⚜ ⚜

Scenic Value: ⚜ ⚜ · Amenities Nearby: ⚜ ⚜ – ⚜ ⚜ ⚜

FEATURED ITEMS

furniture, paintings, statues, lamps, silver, crystal,
jewelry, clothing accessories, stamps, coins, militaria, dolls,
toys, cameras, watches, high-end rustic items

MARKET DETAILS

The Puces de Saint-Ouen describes the 12 separate markets—Antica, Biron, Cambo, Dauphine, Jules Vallès, Malassis, Malik, Michelet, Paul Bert, Rosiers, Serpette and Vernaison—that together make up the giant flea market above the Porte de Clignancourt, at the northern edge of Paris, open to the public on Saturday, Sunday and Monday. These permanent markets generally open between 8 and 9 a.m. on Saturday, 10 a.m. on Sunday and 11 a.m. on Monday, and close around 6 p.m. on Saturday and Sunday (and between 5 and 6 p.m. on Monday).

I F ARRIVING BY PUBLIC TRANSIT, TAKE MÉTRO LINE 4 (PORTE D'ORLÉANS—PORTE DE CLIGNANCOURT), EXITING AT THE PORTE DE CLIGNANCOURT STOP. AS YOU exit you will see signs directing you to the market. (In any event, follow signs for boulevard Ornano, *numéros impairs* (odd numbers), and signs for rue Belliard and boulevard Ney.) Outside, head north on the avenue de la Porte de Clignancourt, which crosses the rue René Binet and passes under the *boulevard périphérique*. The market begins here, in the large area northwest of the intersection of the avenue Michelet (the northern continuation of the avenue de la Porte de Clignancourt) and the rue Jean Henri Fabre (just north of, and parallel to, the *boulevard périphérique*).

The exact addresses of the individual markets are as follows: Antica (99, rue des Rosiers), Biron (85, rue des Rosiers), Cambo (75, rue des Rosiers), Dauphine (140, rue des Rosiers), Jules Vallès (7 to 9, rue Jules Vallès), Malassis (142, rue des Rosiers), Malik (53, rue Jules Vallès), Michelet (avenue Michelet, even numbers), Paul Bert (18, rue Paul Bert), Rosiers (3, rue Paul Bert), Serpette (110, rue des Rosiers) and Vernaison (99, rue des Rosiers).

Originating in the late nineteenth century, when they could truly be called *puces*, the Puces de Saint-Ouen (also referred to as the Porte de Clignancourt flea market) were established as permanent markets beginning in the early twentieth century, just after World War I. Some of the individual markets here consist simply of rows of squat, ramshackle structures, while others are modern brick buildings. Today, they are more similar to antique centers—with vendors allocated separate, permanent, stalls—than to the typical French flea market, where vendors set up, and pack up, each day. The dealers here have small boutiques, which they can simply lock up at the end of the weekend (or Monday evening) and open up again a few days later.

While there is a fair overlap in the kinds of goods sold in each of the individual markets, they have their distinctive flavors. For example, while at Vernaison and Paul Bert you are more likely to find small collectibles and more rustic items (albeit high-end), at Serpette and Biron you will see larger pieces—like furniture, lamps, paintings and bronzes. And, while the appearance of some of the markets—notably, Vernaison and Paul Bert—is quaintly ramshackle, others, like Malassis and Dauphine, are modern and institutional looking.

Whether really *puces* (narrowly defined) or not, the markets that make up the Puces de Saint-Ouen are of enormous importance to the antiques and collectibles trade in France. They also offer an extraordinary opportunity for visitors to see French collectibles at their best, and in all their variety. You will find everything here, from exotic stuffed animals to every possible pattern of *café au lait* bowl. The advantage of the permanent stalls is that they promote specialization by vendors, and the collection of very high-quality wares. And, whatever appeals to you—be it buttons, fabrics, crystal, silver, 60s chrome, copperware, wine collectibles, canes, dolls, rustic garden ware, Art Deco, enamel coffee pots—you will find a vendor here devoted to it, in all of its manifestations and variations.

But do not be led astray by the charmingly haphazard surroundings of some of the markets, and the less than appealing environs. This is fairly uniformly high-quality merchandise, amassed by seasoned vendors who know the value of their wares and who hope to get a good price for them. Their clientele is often other dealers, both from France and abroad—interior decorators from New York and London, for example, with big budgets—rather than casual purchasers. In other words, this is not the place to come if you think you are going to unearth a treasure at a great price.

On the other hand, if you are looking for a particular collectible and are willing to pay for it, this is certainly well worth a visit. The advantage of specialized dealers with high-quality wares, of course, is that you could find something really special here.

Seven markets are featured below, as a representative sampling— Vernaison, Paul Bert, and Biron (whose ambiance and collectibles will perhaps appeal most to casual visitors and collectors), as well as Malassis, Dauphine, Serpette and Jules-Vallès.

MARCHÉ VERNAISON *(99, rue des Rosiers)*

The Marché Vernaison is the most charming of the Porte de Clignancourt markets, and the one which most corresponds to what visitors imagine when they think of French flea markets. Unlike most of its counterparts, it has a real ambiance, with its narrow, meandering laneways lined with tiny boutiques stuffed with collectibles. You could easily get lost wandering around this mostly open-air, triangular space, bordered by the rue des Rosiers, the rue Voltaire and avenue Michelet. If you do, the area is not large, and the experience will be an altogether pleasant one. This is by far my favorite of the Porte de Clignancourt markets, and the one which may appeal most to general tourists and collectors looking to find a small memento of their trip to France.

The shabby charm of Vernaison owes much to its origins and vintage. This is the oldest of the permanent markets, established just after the end of the First World War by a landowner in Saint-Ouen named Romain Vernaison, who set up some pre-fabricated huts here for vendors to sell their wares. Today the market houses about 250 stalls, selling mostly small, everyday collectibles, rather than ornate, decorative

pieces. Here, you will find a wide variety of things, including linens, lace, jewelry, kitchenware, toys, books, clocks, watches, lamps, tapestries and some silver.

MARCHÉ PAUL BERT *(18, rue Paul Bert)*

My second favorite of the Saint-Ouen markets is Paul Bert, which dates from just after World War II. The market's original, primitive stalls were apparently replaced by more solid and permanent-looking structures in the mid 50s. Like Vernaison, this market—with entrances off the rue Paul Bert and the rue des Rosiers—has a kind of homey, comfortable feel, with its rows lined with stalls. There is a pleasant, village-like ambiance here, with vendors standing outside their stalls chatting to each other, and to customers.

But don't be fooled by the casual scene. This is a high-end market, with prices to match. You will see some furniture here, but also ceramics, copperware, garden items and accessories and interesting architectural pieces. I would describe this market as appealing to trendy, rustic tastes, as opposed to those looking for more formal, decorative and classic antiques. One really impressive boutique is Bachelier Antiquités at Allée 1, stand 17, where you will find wonderful warm-toned ceramics, gleaming copper pots and wine collectibles, as well as baskets and garden implements—everyday French kitchen- and gardenware at its finest.

MARCHÉ BIRON *(85, rue des Rosiers)*

Having opened in 1925, the Marché Biron is one of the oldest of the St. Ouen markets. It is also a substantial one, running in two long rows from the rue des Rosiers to the avenue Michelet. One side is open air (like Vernaison and Paul Bert), while the other is covered. The covered side features fairly large boutiques, decorated like rooms and displaying formal, serious antiques, including lots of furniture, while the open-air side offers paintings, lamps, bronzes and fine decorative pieces (silver, glassware and china, posters, scientific and marine objects). It is not surprising that this market once had the nickname, the Faubourg Saint-Honoré des Puces.

MARCHÉ MALASSIS *(142, rue des Rosiers)*

You have to wonder what the people who built this building in the late 80s were thinking. This modern brick structure, which would make a fine suburban mall or office building, utterly lacks the kind of haphazard sprawling charm one comes to expect, and hope for, in a flea market. Having said that, the building does have its attractions, including lots of greenery and well-positioned glass ceilings that provide some welcome natural light. Several dozen vendors have their boutiques in this two-storey building, offering a wide variety of high-end collectibles. They generally specialize in a few select items—furniture, Asian art, carpets, paintings, toys, cameras, high-end kitchenware, marine and scientific objects, books and more.

MARCHÉ DAUPHINE *(140, rue des Rosiers)*

The Marché Dauphine was opened in 1991, two years after the Marché Malassis next door, and is similarly modern and institutional-looking. The two-storey structure is in red brick with green metalwork. This market offers high-end goods of a wide variety—books, watches, clocks, toys, dolls, cameras, jewelry and some furniture. While this is not the place to go if you are looking for a bargain, if money is not a primary concern, you could find a nice transportable memento of your trip here.

MARCHÉ SERPETTE *(110, rue des Rosiers)*

Located next to the Marché Paul Bert, and bordered by the rue des Rosiers and the rue Paul Bert, is the Marché Serpette. Of much greater interest to designers and decorators than casual browsers, this market features mostly high-end furniture and large decorative items—like trunks, mirrors, lamps and statues, with a focus on the period from the late nineteenth century to the 1940s. You will see well-dressed vendors standing around talking to equally well-dressed clients—hardly your typical French flea market scene. But the building has a kind of comfortable feel, despite the rather intimidating nature of its occupants.

MARCHÉ JULES-VALLÈS *(7 to 9, rue Jules Vallès)*

The small Marché Jules-Vallès is one of the oldest markets at the Puces de Saint-Ouen, dating back to 1938. This U-shaped covered space, with stalls in two aisles on either side, is located on the rue Jules Vallès, just east of the rue Lecuyer and west of the rue des Rosiers. The last time I was here I noticed religious objects, militaria, china and advertising items, among other collectibles.

OTHER THINGS TO DO

It can be a rather exhausting experience to visit the Puces de Saint-Ouen flea markets, so you may wish to stop off for a drink or a light meal before heading back to the center of Paris. For a place in keeping with the markets' vintage focus, check out Chez Louisette (tel. 01-40-12-10-14), tucked away in the alleyways of the Marché Vernaison. This is reputed to be where the legendary Edith Piaf began her great singing career. The atmosphere here is pleasant and comfortable, though the food is not spectacular or particularly inexpensive.

For more interesting fare, and more aesthetic surroundings, try Le Paul Bert (20, rue Paul Bert, tel. 01-40-11-90-28). Another popular spot is Le Biron, at the entrance to the Marché Biron (85, rue des Rosiers, tel. 01-40-12-65-65), while tiny La Chope des Puces (122, rue des Rosiers, tel. 01-40-11-02-49) also offers live guitar music on weekend afternoons.

PORTE DE MONTREUIL
Saturday, Sunday & Monday

Number of Vendors: 50 ("puces" vendors) · Price - Quality: ⚜

Scenic Value: ⚜ · Amenities Nearby: ⚜ – ⚜ ⚜

FEATURED ITEMS

hardware, tools, kitchenware, bric-a-brac

MARKET DETAILS

The Porte de Montreuil market (where mostly new items are sold) is held in the east end of Paris, on Saturday, Sunday and Monday. If arriving by public transit, take *métro* line 9 (Pont de Sèvres—Mairie de Montreuil) and get off at the Porte de Montreuil stop. As you are leaving the station, follow signs for avenue de la Mairie de Montreuil, *numéros impairs* (odd numbers), and then go east to the place de la Porte de Montreuil. Cross the square (just above the *boulevard périphérique*) and then turn left (north) on the avenue du Professeur André Lemierre. You will find a few collectibles stalls interspersed here, but the majority are located at the far end of the market.

THE PORTE DE MONTREUIL MARKET IS ONE I WOULD ONLY RECOMMEND TO THE MOST INTREPID FLEA MARKETER: A PERSON WHO DOESN'T MIND traveling to one of the more unscenic parts of Paris to wade though seemingly endless stalls of cheap new goods—or a lot of junk—in the slim hope of finding a treasure. Even this pursuit has become increasingly difficult, as the number of collectibles vendors seems to have diminished over the last few years. Nonetheless, collectors' magazines still include the Porte de Montreuil in their lists of French flea markets, and people continue to come here in search of a bargain. And, you never know, you could be one of the lucky few to depart with a little treasure purchased here for only a few euros.

The setting of this market is especially unappealing. It is true that the other two Parisian flea markets—the Porte de Vanves and the Puces de Saint-Ouen—are also located by the *boulevard périphérique* that encircles Paris, but the Porte de Montreuil market is, in my view, the most unattractive. As you exit the *métro* station, and head toward the vast arid space by the highway that houses the market, you will wonder why you have bothered to come. Passing through the maze of stalls selling cheap sunglasses, umbrellas, t-shirts and shoes, you will also wonder whether there are any collectibles to be found.

And then, you will begin to spot them here and there—bits of crockery, pots and pans, glassware and utensils, even a few decorative pieces, and perhaps an appealing *café au lait* bowl or enamel coffee pot. Most of what you see will be of little interest from a collectibles point of view, but the upside is that if you do spot something interesting, you will be able to purchase it for a fraction of the price at other markets.

At the very end of the market, along the avenue du Professeur André Lemierre, there is a section devoted specifically to *puces*, broadly defined. In this small rabbit-warren of tables piled high with what looks almost entirely like junk, you will find vendors selling books, tools, hardware and some everyday kitchenware—old ceramic pieces, dishware from the 50s, old pots and pans. Again, there may be some interesting finds to be had, especially for those who collect everyday items and rustic ware, but the search will involve ferreting through a lot of junk in the process. The last time I was here I have to confess that I spotted very little of interest, and my tastes run to the distinctly rustic, as opposed to finer decorative pieces.

OTHER THINGS TO DO

The chances of you wanting to hang around this part of Paris after visiting the flea market are slim indeed. However, for bargain hunters interested in everyday objects, there is a well-stocked, inexpensive and interesting charity shop, just a few stops further east on the *métro*, at the Mairie de Montreuil *métro* stop. Called Le Radeau Neptune, it is located at 32, boulevard Paul Vaillant Couturier, less than a ten-minute walk from the station. The shop is open Tuesday to Saturday, from 9 a.m. to 12:30 p.m. and 2 p.m. to 6 p.m., and Sunday from 2 p.m. to 6 p.m. However, call ahead to confirm the hours before you go (tel. 01-48-51-54-62).

Also on *métro* line 9, but at the other end of Paris, near the Jasmin *métro* stop, is a smaller, but somewhat interesting, charity shop (in a much more tony neighborhood), called Les Orphelins Apprentis d'Auteuil (40, rue la Fontaine). Its hours are Monday to Friday, 2:30 p.m. to 6 p.m., September to mid-July, but, again, call ahead to confirm (tel. 01-44-14-76-79).

PORTE DE VANVES
Saturday & Sunday morning

Number of Vendors: 380 · Price-Quality: ✤ ✤ – ✤ ✤ ✤
Scenic Value: ✤ – ✤ ✤ · Amenities Nearby: ✤ ✤

FEATURED ITEMS

ceramics, porcelain, glassware, linens, paintings and prints,
militaria, Art Deco, silver, clocks, lamps, books, copperware,
secondhand clothing, some furniture

MARKET DETAILS

The Porte de Vanves flea market is held on Saturday and Sunday morning, in the
south end of Paris, along the avenue Marc Sangnier and the adjacent avenue Georges
Lafenestre. While a few vendors stay later (on the avenue G. Lafenestre), most pack
up around 1 p.m., so make sure to come in the morning. If arriving by public transit,
take *métro* line 13 [St. Denis-Université or Gabriel Péri (Asnières-Gennevilliers)—
Chatillon-Montrouge] to the Porte de Vanves stop; the market is just a couple of
minutes' walk from here. Follow signs for avenue Marc Sangnier as you exit the station. You should find yourself on the boulevard Brune; just a little further west you

will come to the place de la Porte de Vanves. Turn left (south) and the avenue Marc Sangnier is the first street south.

THE PORTE DE VANVES FLEA MARKET IS WITHOUT A DOUBT ONE OF THE BEST IN FRANCE, IN TERMS OF SIZE, QUALITY AND VARIETY. ITS SETTING, THOUGH not attractive, is the least unappealing of the three big flea markets in Paris. Like the Porte de Montreuil and Porte de Clignancourt (Puces de Saint-Ouen) markets, it is held at the edge of the city, alongside the *boulevard périphérique*. However, the market's immediate environs are fairly pleasant; the stalls stretch out along a quiet avenue lined with trees, mostly out of view of the unsightly, and busy, road nearby.

The Porte de Vanves market encapsulates the French flea market at its best. Not only is it very significant in size, with around 380 vendors, the wares for sale run a wide gamut in terms of price and variety. You can pick up something interesting for just a few euros, or splurge on a special decorative piece for a few hundred euros. The market also boasts a wide range in terms of the provenance of the goods; for example, you will see ceramics from Alsace and Brittany, alongside pieces from the Pays Basque, the Savoie and Provence. You will also find collectibles from other parts of Europe, as well as from North America and Asia (not surprising, given Paris's international stature, but welcome indeed).

The Porte de Vanves is also exactly what a flea market should be, in terms of the turnover of the merchandise. One weekend, for example, you may detect a focus on Art Deco (on the part of a few vendors), while the next you may be drawn to 60s and 70s furniture and accessories. And, while there are dealers who specialize in particular things, there are also others who appear to set out whatever they have picked up

during the week. As a result, this is one of those markets that collectors staying in Paris for a period of time will want to check out on a regular basis.

This is a very busy market indeed and one worth arriving at early if you hope to make a great find. Give yourself a couple of hours to wend your way along the stalls—there is such a feast for the eyes here that you will want to have time to absorb it all. The clientele is a happy mix of Parisians and tourists from all over the world and the atmosphere is pleasant and relaxed. While I would not describe vendors as wildly friendly and talkative, many will speak at least some English. Also, a certain amount of bargaining is both expected and welcomed.

If you have only a short time to spend in Paris—and can only take in one flea market—this is the one I would recommend, unless you are a serious and well-heeled antiques collector or dealer, in which case the Porte de Clignancourt may be your destination of choice.

OTHER THINGS TO DO

There are a couple of food vendors interspersed among the stalls where you can pick up a drink or a snack as you wander along. And, if you are in desperate need of a café after checking out the market, there are a couple back toward the *métro*, on the boulevard Brune, near the avenue G. Lafenestre. Otherwise, your best bet is to head to the far more visually appealing center of Paris.

OTHER PARISIAN MARKETS

A small number of bric-a-brac vendors offer their eclectic wares at the place d'Aligre market, held every morning except Monday in the twelfth arrondissement, near the Lédru-Rollin *métro* stop on Line 8. This market is of some interest to bargain-hunters (not general tourists), and even then it can be quite disappointing. In the past, I have found a few interesting things here, but much less so in recent years. However, the produce in the adjacent food market is excellent and inexpensive. And, right nearby, at 5 place d'Aligre, is a great bakery selling fine *pain biologique* (organic bread), called Boulangerie le Pain au Naturel Moisan (with a number of other outlets in the city as well).

THE

Flea Markets

of

PROVENCE

THE

Flea Markets

of

PROVENCE

⚜

ABOUT THE REGION

PROVENCE IS OFTEN WHAT FIRST COMES TO MIND WHEN PEOPLE CONJURE UP IMAGES OF AN IDYLLIC FRENCH COUNTRYSIDE. SEVERAL DISPARATE forces—from the Impressionists to Peter Mayle—have contributed to cementing this region in our collective imaginations. But Provence also manages to live up to its billing, particularly on a sunny day, while driving through vineyards or sitting under the shade of tall plane trees surrounded by pale stone buildings with pastel shutters.

Not brilliantly colorful and showy like the Côte d'Azur, Provence has that wonderful languid quality that makes it so appealing as a place to spend time. A number of influences combine to work its magic—long vistas of lavender fields, olive groves punctuated by mountains and rocky ridges, sleepy villages with peaceful squares, a big pale blue sky and a feeling of space and tranquility, despite all the tourists who come here. Even the larger towns and cities in this largely rural region—Arles, Avignon and Aix-en-Provence, for example—exude that very Provençal feel.

I have spent a number of years in this region—based in Haute Provence—just northwest of the Mont Ventoux. We lived in a sixteenth-century stone building, in a valley overlooking vineyards, fruit trees and a thousand-year-old ruin. Our children attended the one-room school across the way, and on their return home would be waylaid by our 80-year-old neighbor, who would offer them snakes and games he had carved out of bamboo shoots. The farmer next door would leave boxes of ripe melons and plump cherries by our gate. On market days, we would head with our baskets to Vaison-la-Romaine, Carpentras and Nyons to buy food, but also simply revel in the scene around us.

It was during those years that I first became drawn to the flea markets in France. On weekends, we would head out early in search of treasures, to both low-end and more high-end markets—in places like Jonquières, Mornas, Montfavet, Avignon, Villeneuve-lès-Avignon, L'Isle-sur-la-Sorgue and Aix-en-Provence. Most I only heard about through word-of-mouth, so that when we would travel further afield it was harder to find out where they were.

It was also just through rifling though the wares week after week that I came to learn about the wonderful variety—and regional diversity—of collectibles in France. I also came to appreciate—as the French deeply do—that the simplest, most rustic, everyday object can be enormously appealing, and your favorite treasure. Living in Provence, where objects with a patina and wear are cherished—not just for their appearance but for what they say about the way of life they represent—made that discovery all the more easy.

ABOUT THE MARKETS

Provence boasts many very colorful and lively outdoor food markets—perhaps the best in France. It also has some of the country's finest flea markets. These are often substantial and animated events, which operate at a brisk pace year round (despite some blustery days, when the infamous wind, the Mistral, blows down the Rhône valley). People come here for the fun of visiting the flea markets in this region. But, more importantly, they come here to buy—to purchase some of the many collectibles that so typify this part of France. Like the region itself, the Provençal style stirs imaginations worldwide; to many collectors, decorators and designers it embodies all that is most appealing in the French way of life.

And the flea markets are a great source for Provençal collectibles. The focus here is on rustic, functional, everyday objects, with that essential emblem of authenticity —wear. Distressed café tables and metal chairs with wooden slats, busy Provençal fabrics and quilts (called *boutis*), wooden and iron tools, enamel coffee pots, *café au lait* bowls, old *boules* (in nail-studded wood or bronze), *santons* (the traditional ceramic Provençal figures in regional dress), baskets, metal bottle carriers, wooden shoes and crisp linens are just some of the things you will find here. Provençal ceramics in earthy tones, as opposed to fine porcelain, are very popular, as is pewter, perhaps more than silver. Old terra cotta garden pots, wrought-iron plant holders and garden accessories generally are in big demand in this place of outdoor living. And farming implements of all kinds, as well as wine collectibles, are another major feature of these markets, not surprising given the rural roots of this region.

Another great thing about the flea markets of Provence is that there is a wide range in the levels of markets and in the prices of the collectibles. At the higher end is the renowned L'Isle-sur-la-Sorgue market, where the goods are well-edited, well-polished and beautifully displayed. Toward the middle of the range is the lively market in Carpentras, where many of the vendors appear to be ordinary people keen to empty out the *grenier* and make a few euros in the process. And there are more basic markets yet—like Montfavet and Mornas—places lacking in touristic appeal, but where some real bargains can be found.

There is a unifying thread that runs through these markets, though, whether the wares are high-end or more modest. These are unpretentious, down-home affairs (even if sometimes consciously so), where a back-to-basics, down-to-earth approach is extolled. In brilliant sunshine, alleviated by leafy plane trees, these markets are elemental, rather than ornate. Simplicity dominates here—not fussiness—in both the look and wares in these markets.

Though elemental markets of the *terroir*, you will not feel the least bit out of place here. While not consciously catering to tourists (L'Isle-sur-la-Sorgue, perhaps, is an exception), there is a recognition that tourism is a big fact of life in Provence, and that many of the markets' customers, especially during the summer months, are foreigners. If you do not speak French well, no one will be surprised, so do not hesitate to throw yourself in with everyone around you in *la chine*. And that includes bargaining, which is practiced seriously and with enthusiasm here.

WHEN TO GO ✦ HOW TO TRAVEL

While the flea markets in Provence are busy year-round, the winter is not the best season to visit here. Early morning temperatures are chilly then, even if it warms up substantially during the day, and if there is a Mistral the markets can be frigid. (It is not unusual to encounter frost on the ground, and an early morning fog, driving to the markets on crisp winter mornings.) The late spring and early fall are probably the best times to come, since the summer can be oppressively hot and dry (with not a lot of water around), and the markets crowded.

As for the best mode of transportation, train travel can be difficult here. Several of the places (and markets) you will want to visit are not accessible by train, and not easily accessible by bus, either. Having a car is very useful, especially since one of your primary objectives will be touring the Provençal countryside. And, while driving can be surprisingly tricky, especially on some of the small narrow roads, they usually are not crowded.

ARLES
First Wednesday
of the month

Number of Vendors: 80 to 100 · Price-Quality: ⚜ ⚜ ⚜
Scenic Value: ⚜ ⚜ – ⚜ ⚜ ⚜ · Amenities Nearby: ⚜ ⚜ – ⚜ ⚜ ⚜

FEATURED ITEMS

Provençal clothing and accessories, lace, regional ceramics, tools,
books, some furniture, rustic items generally

MARKET DETAILS

The Arles flea market takes place all day, on the first Wednesday of the month, along
the boulevard des Lices at the southern edge of town. If arriving by car, you should
be able to find metered parking further along the street. If arriving by train, it is
about a 20-minute walk to the market. Go south on the avenue Talbot to the end,
and continue south (after a little jog to the east) on the rue Voltaire to the Arena.
At its southern end, take the rue Porte de Laure to the Jardin d'Été. The market is at
its bottom end.

ARLES HAS A SURREAL QUALITY THAT IS HINTED AT, THOUGH IN A LESS INTENSE
WAY, THROUGHOUT PROVENCE. PERHAPS IT IS THE LUMINOUS QUALITY OF
the light—gentle, as opposed to crisp—reflecting off its pale ancient

buildings and exuding a kind of langorous, bucolic feel. The effect is mesmerizing, though I must admit that I find it somewhat disconcerting and energy-sapping, particularly in the heat of summer.

There is a sense of timelessness which infuses this town. Certainly, Arles has its share of modern boutiques and amenities, but it is its historic sites—primarily, of course, its 2,000-year-old arena—which dominate the space, and seem to keep Arles somewhat insulated from the modernizing influences all around it. One cannot help but feel transported by even a short visit to this place.

History has had a huge role to play here. The town was a major hub during the Roman Empire, and again during the Middle Ages. However, Arles has lost some of its prominence over the last few centuries, to more vibrant places like Avignon and Aix-en-Provence. One thing it does firmly retain, though, is its image as the chronicler and protector of Provençal culture and heritage. The great Frédéric Mistral, so synonymous with that quest, created the Museon Arlaten in Arles at the end of the nineteenth century, to showcase, and celebrate, those traditions.

THE MARKET

The flea market, which takes place all day on the first Wednesday of the month along the boulevard des Lices, bears testimony to Arles's ties to its Provençal culture and past. With about 80 vendors, this is a substantial market, firmly rooted in the *terroir*—from the Camargue in the south to the rugged ridges to the north. While there are many collectibles here from other regions of France, Provence and its way of life predominate.

Perhaps the first thing you notice as you stroll by the tables set up in two long

rows along the boulevard is the number of booths specializing in traditional Arlesian clothing and accessories—black vests with white cotton blouses, short fitted jackets, full white underskirts, colorful shawls and old black cotton umbrellas, as well as fine lacework and ribbons and lovely beaded purses. The region is also evoked in collectibles for the home—old wooden caned chairs, small wooden cupboards lined with mesh to store bread (called *panetières*), and iron door knockers shaped like bulls' heads (reflecting the Camargue, of course). Rustic tools, milk jugs, cow bells and large copper pots all testify to the strong rural, practical roots of this region, while the ceramic *santons* in Provençal clothing, bronze and nail-studded *boules* and decorative ceramic *cigales* recall the more whimsical side of its character.

Like the town itself, there is a calm, laid-back quality to this market. Prices are not low (though I found the linens, for example, to be quite reasonable), but vendors will bargain and are receptive to and familiar with foreigners. This is a market I would try to include in your itinerary if you are in the area. While the setting is not particularly beautiful, it is a pleasant way to spend an hour or so while in Arles, and it will provide some real insight into everyday life in this region in decades past.

OTHER THINGS TO DO

Another great way to get a glimpse of the cultural history of the area is to visit the nearby Museon Arlaten (29, rue de la République, tel. 04-90-93-58-11), which focuses on the rituals and practices of everyday life in this region. For a flavorful and reasonably priced lunch in very pleasant surroundings, try Le 16 (16, rue du Docteur Fanton, tel. 04-90-93-77-36). In this tastefully decorated restaurant with beamed ceilings, the solid wooden tables are set with colorful cloths and the food is nicely prepared and equally well-presented.

If you are heading north toward Avignon, be sure to stop in at St. Rémy-de-Provence, with its many antique and home décor stores. And Tarascon, to the west of St. Rémy and north of Arles, is the headquarters of the well-known fabric and design company, Souleiado (39, rue Proudhon), which also offers visits to its impressive museum of Provençal fabrics and culture, the Musée du Tissu Provençal Souleiado (tel. 04-90-91-50-11). Here you will see examples of the wood blocks used to make the *indiennes* prints, as well as some fine old *boutis*, the traditional Provençal quilts.

OTHER NEARBY MARKETS

A modest-sized flea market takes place in Aix-en-Provence (about 45 minutes' drive east of Arles), as part of its general market, on Tuesday, Thursday and Saturday morning, in the place de Verdun, in front of the Palais de Justice. Nîmes (about 30 minutes west) has a moderate-sized flea market on Mondays, all day, along the avenue Jean Jaurès.

AVIGNON

Saturday morning

Number of Vendors: 40 · Price - Quality: ⚜ ⚜ – ⚜ ⚜ ⚜
Scenic Value: ⚜ ⚜ ⚜ – ⚜ ⚜ ⚜ · Amenities Nearby: ⚜ ⚜

FEATURED ITEMS

ceramics, baskets, tools, agricultural implements, garden pots and accessories, boutis (colorful Provençal quilts), trunks, linens, pewter, glassware,
porcelain, kitchenware, lamps, fireplace accessories, furniture,
50s and 60s collectibles, paintings, books

MARKET DETAILS

The Villeneuve-lès-Avignon flea market takes place on Saturday morning, just across
the Rhône from Avignon, in the place Charles David at the edge of this small town. If
arriving by car, from the road circling Avignon's ramparts follow signs to Villeneuve-lès-
Avignon. Once you cross the Rhône, follow the sign for Villeneuve indicating a turn toward the right. About a kilometer along the avenue de Verdun, you will come upon the
market by the side of the road. It takes place here and in the adjacent place Charles David
(also called the place du Marché). Getting here without a car is more difficult; ask for
information on bus routes at Avignon's Office de Tourisme on the rue de la République.

AVIGNON HAS BOTH THE ADVANTAGE AND DISADVANTAGE OF BEING CIR-CUMSCRIBED BY ITS IMPRESSIVE FOURTEENTH-CENTURY RAMPARTS. THEY preserve the integrity of the city's extraordinary architectural heritage and prevent expansion; they also preclude any initiative to add some much-needed green space to this city's dense core.

Avignon has a distinguished past—its heyday was during the fourteenth century, when the popes set up operations here for several decades and occupied the remarkable Palais des Papes. In a way, though, that past has weighed heavily on the town, at least until recently. When I first came here 20 years ago, I found the city closed and conservative-feeling, lacking the liveliness of nearby Aix, for example. During the day the streets were busy with shoppers, but at night the city seemed almost eerily quiet and deserted.

On my most recent visit, however, things seemed much changed. The city feels brighter, more open now. Buildings have been restored and scrubbed clean, making them lighter, more airy. The new openness is also literally true. Giant museum doors have been thrown open to the outside world, inviting passersby in and offering glimpses of the architectural marvels inside. The place des Corps Saints next to the tourist office has been renovated with a similar approach. Combining the elegance of the classical with the lightness of modernity seems to be the underlying premise of Avignon's revitalization.

Villeneuve-lès-Avignon, just across the Rhône (and technically part of Languedoc-Roussillon, not Provence), was a fortress town during the Middle Ages, as its imposing Tour Philippe-le-Bel and the gigantic Fort SaintAndré attest. It also became a kind of suburban refuge for church cardinals who built villas here. Today, this quiet

enclave, in the shadow of Avignon, provides a welcome break from the more crowded scene on the other side of the Rhône.

THE MARKET

Villeneuve-lès-Avignon's Saturday flea market is one of the best in Provence, and one of my favorite haunts when I lived in this region. It has something for everyone—rustic, regional collectibles and finer decorative items. Prices also run the gamut; you can find something for a couple of euros or a couple of hundred euros. Some vendors concentrate on particular items (well selected and also more expensive) while others arrive with boxes filled with crockery and everyday household goods that they likely picked up in some old shed or *grenier*.

This is a big market, with around 100 vendors filling the place Charles David and spilling onto the adjacent avenue de Verdun. While not stunning, the setting is pleasing, overlooked by the massive medieval Fort Saint-André. In a corner is a little outdoor café and also a vendor selling oysters, sea urchins and shrimp. (Well before lunchtime you will see plates of empty oyster shells on vendors' tables. Their day started very early, after all.) The only thing that risks disturbing the bustling tranquility (contradictory, but true) of this place is the infamous Mistral, which races down the Rhône, especially on clear sunny days. I have seen it suddenly lift dishes and glassware from vendors' tables and send them crashing to the ground.

This is a market collectors will love, for a simple reason. They stand a very good chance of finding something interesting here at a reasonable price. Vendors are cautiously friendly (in typical Provençal fashion) and expect you to bargain. If they name a price and you remain silent, they may well then lower it themselves. There is a wide variety of collectibles, but with an emphasis on the rustic Provençal items so sought after by locals and visitors alike—lovely green and yellow glazed ceramic pots, Provençal quilts, garden pots and accessories, metal bottle carriers, copper pots, baskets, forged-iron tools, agricultural implements (bells, harnesses) and more. You will, however, also find more formal decorative items—porcelain, crystal and paintings, for example. Linens abound, as do lamps, hardware and fixtures, fireplace accessories and furniture.

Despite its regional focus, this is a good market for finding ceramics from other parts of France—dishware from Limoges, folkloric Quimper ware and ceramics from the Côte d'Azur, for example. The last time I was here I bought two very old green and brown glazed bowls from Vallauris for just two euros each.

Another departure from the focus on Provence is the increasing presence of collectibles from the 60s and 70s—chrome lamps and accessories, volcanic-looking ceramics and plastic in bright colors. Apparently, here as elsewhere in France, younger people are increasingly drawn to relics of that era. Strangely, these items co-exist reasonably well with the traditional Provençal collectibles in this market.

This is a market worth arriving at early, if you can. Things get snapped up quickly as I was reminded the last time I came. Enthralled with a grimy but beautiful *café au lait* bowl decorated with birds, I moved on briefly, because the vendor was absent from his stall. When I returned a couple of minutes later, the bowl was gone. If you see something you like here, don't hesitate; chances are that someone else will come along and scoop it up.

OTHER THINGS TO DO

Once you have finished browsing the market, you may wish to head back into Avignon and check out the sites. The city has a number of chic restaurants (whose décor combines the classic and the modern, like Avignon's own renovation project). One is La Compagnie des Comptoirs (83, rue Joseph Vernet, tel. 04-90-85-99-04), serving French fusion cuisine.

At the other end of the spectrum, but offering great value and very popular with the locals, is Maison Nani (29, rue Théodore Aubanel , tel. 04-90-82-60-90), just off the central rue de la République. This friendly place, which calls itself *le restaurant des Avignonnais*, is jammed at lunchtime—families with babies, grandmothers, dogs—and the owner seems to know them all. The food is not fancy, but is nicely prepared, with generous salads and reasonably-priced *steak frites*.

If you just want a good baguette sandwich to eat on the run, a great bet is Le Fournil des Papes, a bakery at 45, cours Jean Jaurès, the lower extension of the rue de la République (the sign says "Maître Panisse"). The sandwiches are fresh, the bread is good and you can eat your lunch in the stunning square just up the street, next to the Office de Tourisme.

OTHER NEARBY MARKETS

Avignon itself has a real *puces* market on Sunday mornings at the place des Carmes, in the center of town, which will be of some interest to bargain hunters (not general tourists). On Tuesdays and Thursdays, a small *brocante* market takes place in the place Pie (until early afternoon). If you are a really hardened bargain hunter, interested in everyday items and willing to scrounge through piles of secondhand junk, Montfavet, a few kilometers east of Avignon, has a fairly large Saturday morning market, in the Quartier Bompas, route de Marseille.

CARPENTRAS
Sunday

Number of Vendors: 130 to 150 · Price-Quality: ⚜⚜–⚜⚜⚜
Scenic Value: ⚜⚜ · Amenities Nearby: ⚜⚜

FEATURED ITEMS

kitchenware, enamelware, advertising items (pitchers and ashtrays, etc.), copperware, glassware, cameras, linens, tools, garden items, baskets, regional ceramics, porcelain, paintings, santons (Provençal figures), Epiphany fèves (small ceramic objects hidden in the galettes des rois cakes during Epiphany), boutis (Provençal quilts), books

MARKET DETAILS

The Carpentras flea market takes place all day (from mid-morning to late afternoon) on Sunday, in the parking lot des Platanes in the center of town. If arriving by car, the site is between the place Aristide Briand and the place de Verdun, alongside the avenue Jean Jaurès, a main street that edges the town on the east.

CARPENTRAS—LOCATED ABOUT 20 KILOMETERS TO THE NORTHEAST OF AVIGNON—IS A STRANGE, BUT INTERESTING TOWN. ITS ORIGINS ARE EXTREMELY OLD, dating back over 2,000 years ago. For a short time during the fourteenth

century, it served as the papal center, and because of the protection given to Jews by the Church, Carpentras boasts a synagogue from this period, apparently the oldest in France (among those still in existence).

In recent years, Carpentras has been in the process of some much-needed revitalization. But new projects aside, some of the narrow dark streets in the center look less than inviting, particularly after dark. Even midday on Sunday, the town core feels quite deserted (in stark contrast to the lively flea market in full swing a few blocks away). However, on Friday mornings this place is bustling indeed, during the town's wonderful food market, which draws shoppers from across the region.

I see Carpentras as the gateway to Haute Provence—south of here the countryside is quite flat, delineated with rows of tall hedges protecting the fields from the wind. The landscape suddenly opens up leaving town to the north, revealing the more rugged terrain around the towns and villages of Beaumes-de-Venise, Bédoin, Caromb and Le Barroux. The countryside here is particularly spectacular, with vineyards and olive groves framed by the looming specter of the Mont Ventoux on one side and the jagged Dentelles de Montmirail on the other.

THE MARKET

Though lukewarm about the town itself, I am wild about Carpentras's flea market. Of fairly recent vintage (by French flea market standards), this is a large, busy and well-entrenched market, one that draws crowds on a regular basis because they are confident of finding something new and appealing here. Part of the reason is that vendors seem to be regular people (not dealers) who bring along whatever they can find to sell—lots of collectibles, to be sure, but also some secondhand goods.

Prices, as a result, are reasonable, and vendors are noticeably approachable and happy to bargain.

There are up to 150 vendors at this market, who set up either at tables or on the ground, in two long rows spanning the parking lot. The setting is not too bad, thanks in large part to the rows of giant plane trees that line the way. There is a little café truck in the center, offering drinks, sandwiches, *frites* and *crêpes* to the passersby.

Mostly this place is dedicated to the no-nonsense activity of *la chine* (roughly translated, browsing for finds), with all eyes riveted on the wares. You can find just about anything here, though the emphasis is on mid-range, everyday collectibles rather than high-end goods. Luckily, most vendors do not specialize in any particular thing, which means some great deals can be had. Kitchenware of all sorts abounds— *café au lait* bowls, enamel pots, functional ceramics from Provence and elsewhere, copper pots, dishes, utensils, metal bottle carriers, advertising pitchers (Pastis, Pernod, etc.). There are also lots of linens (if not of spectacular quality, reasonably priced), antique tools, gardening accessories (pots, watering cans, utensils), baskets, *boules*, *santons*, *boutis*, paintings, porcelain, pewter, Epiphany *fèves*, cameras, furniture and much else. Some items really stand out. On my last visit I saw two very rare *jaspe* ceramic plates (where the glaze gives a marbled effect) from Apt, about 60 kilometers to the southeast, and a wonderful, colorful plate with the face of a *sanglier* (wild boar) on it.

This is a good market for finding collectibles from other regions of France at a very good price. I recently purchased a brilliantly colorful bowl from Vallauris (near Antibes) for only eight euros, which would have been four times that price in the

Côte d'Azur. That is the beauty of this market—surprises and great finds are much more possible here than in many of the other significant markets in France.

OTHER THINGS TO DO

Carpentras does not have a lot of interesting restaurants, and there is a particular paucity when it comes to those open for Sunday lunch. A notable (and very pleasant) exception, however, is Franck Restaurant (30, place de l'Horloge, tel. 04-90-60-75-00), just a few minutes' walk into the center. The décor in this high-ceilinged, wood-beamed restaurant is surprisingly modern, and the food is inventive and tasty.

Of course, the surrounding countryside abounds with great ideas for things to do. One of my favorite excursions is to drive to nearby Beaumes-de-Venise, renowned for its sweet white Muscat wine (*vin doux*). The most picturesque (and very sought-after) vineyards are those of the Domaine de Durban (tel. 04-90-62-94-26), a few kilometers outside of town (follow signs to the vineyard on the western edge of town). The drive is memorable and the *domaine* itself has stunning views on both sides—toward the Mont Ventoux to the east and the Rhône valley to the west.

From Beaumes-de-Venise heading north, you will pass the picturesque hillside town of Le Barroux. Friends who live there tell me they are very pleased to have a new restaurant close by in Caromb, L'Instant Gourmand (avenue Charles de Gaulle, tel. 04-90-37-19-49)—"*petit, joli et avec un très bon acceuil*" (small, pretty and with a very nice welcome), is how they describe it. My old stomping grounds, Malaucène, a few kilometers further north and west, has a new, much-touted restaurant called Le Pont de l'Orme (route de Suzette, tel. 04-90-46-17-50), near the exit of town heading toward Vaison-la-Romaine, with a very well-priced lunch menu.

Of course, the regular food markets in this part of Provence are not to be missed. Apart from Carpentras's Friday morning one, Vaison-la-Romaine has its great food market on Tuesday morning. On a sunny day, there is no better way to experience Provence than to head to market, pick up some bread, *chèvre* cheese and *saucissons* and have a picnic lunch in the countryside.

OTHER NEARBY MARKETS

Vaison-la-Romaine has a smallish all-day flea market on the third Sunday of the month in the center of town. And, for those bargain-hunters who don't mind a very basic, down-home scene, I suggest heading early in the morning to either Jonquières or Mornas (or maybe both, if you are really keen). Jonquières's market is on Sunday morning, just west of town, while the Mornas market is on both Saturday and Sunday morning alongside the R.N. 7 (between Orange and Bollène). Just a few kilometers north of Carpentras, the village of Bédoin also has a small flea market on Saturday mornings, from the end of March to the end of October, perhaps meriting a look if you are staying nearby.

L'ISLE-SUR-LA-SORGUE

Sunday

Number of Vendors: 40 · Price-Quality: ⚜ ⚜ ⚜ – ⚜ ⚜ ⚜ ⚜
Scenic Value: ⚜ ⚜ ⚜ · Amenities Nearby: ⚜ ⚜ ⚜

FEATURED ITEMS

linens, Provençal pots and ceramics, enamel coffeepots, enamel plaques,
tools, trunks, boules, porcelain, café au lait bowls, paintings, furniture,
santons, colored soda bottles, silver, garden accessories, copperware,
folk art, antique irons, tins, baskets

MARKET DETAILS

L'Isle-sur-la-Sorgue's flea market takes place on Sunday all day along the avenue
des Quatre Otages, in the center of town. Unless you arrive early, parking can be
difficult to find; the best bet is to try one of the side streets leading away from the
market.

O MANY, THE NAME L'ISLE-SUR-LA-SORGUE IS SYNONYMOUS WITH PROVENÇAL
ANTIQUES, AND THE REASON IS CLEAR AS SOON AS YOU START TO ROAM
around here. There are a number of "antiques villages"—enclaves of high-end

antiques dealers—throughout town, and also several stores which specialize in Provençal home décor.

L'Isle-sur-la-Sorgue has a long history in the textile and leather industries, thanks to the many wooden wheels (still present, and now pleasingly covered in moss) which produced power from the several branches of the Sorgue River flowing through town. It is this river that makes L'Isle-sur-la-Sorgue such an agreeable place to be, particularly on a hot summer day when you feel that Provence could certainly do with some more water. Here all is fresh and luxuriant, as you stroll along the little bridges crisscrossing the river, watching the ducks swim by. The vegetation is also wonderfully green, so welcome in this rather arid region.

THE MARKET

In addition to its several *villages antiquaires*, L'Isle-sur-la-Sorgue has a moderate-sized, but high-quality flea market, that takes place Sunday all day along the avenue des Quatre Otages, which edges the old town. The market coincides with the town's lively weekly food market, which is held in the morning in neighboring streets. This is a great place for general tourists as well as collectors; the food market offers a wonderful foray into some of the culinary specialties of the region (olives, *tapenade*, goat cheese, *fougasse*), while the flea market encapsulates the best of *l'art de vivre en Provence*.

Vendors at this market carefully arrange their wares as if they were creating a theatrical set, and in some ways they are. Wood is polished to a fine sheen, linens are tied with pretty ribbons and set out in neat piles, cow bells dangle from special rods,

and enamel coffee pots—all shiny and clean—are set up in groups of colors. A primitive miniature wooden boat, or a basket of gleaming *boules*, is strategically placed on top of a rustic cupboard, just so. Even if you are a bit taken aback by the prices here, you cannot help but admire the taste with which everything is arranged and the magnificent effect it produces.

The prices are quite high, but the quality of the goods is evident. If cost is not a huge factor for you, and your main objective is ensuring that you have found something really authentic, then this is a good market for you. Vendors, who are so accustomed to tourists browsing and not buying, are surprisingly friendly and informative once you engage them in conversation. After I asked one man if I could take photos of his wares, he took me around and pointed out the items he found especially interesting—an old trunk from Metz (in northern France), with the word *curé* (parish priest) on it, and lovely old bottles, used for lemonade, with Carpentras and Orange (nearby towns) etched on them. Several vendors speak quite passable English, and seem to enjoy getting to practice it.

Even if you don't buy anything at this market, you will gain a pretty clear idea of what Provençal décor is all about, and why it has captured the imagination of people all over the world in the last couple of decades. I picked up one of my favorite flea market finds here—an old circular hooked rug, bearing the image of a well-dressed young man smoking a cigarette. Not Provençal perhaps, but fun.

OTHER THINGS TO DO

There are a couple of appealing cafés in town, for a coffee or light snack after seeing the market. Just across the bridge is the aptly-named Au Chineur (esplanade

Robert Vasse), decorated inside and out with flea market finds (there are even old sewing machines perched on the window ledges above, and a vintage tricycle dangling from the café's sign). Another spot to check out is the Bar Petrarque, in the Hotel la Gueulardière, just across the street from the flea market (1, route d'Apt). You will be overwhelmed by all the colorful *cartes scolaires* lining the walls here. (As the owner explained, these old posters, depicting groups of objects—animals, foods, plants—used to hang on school classroom walls.) The hotel's restaurant, also stuffed with collectibles, is amazing as well.

For really good coffee, a wide selection of teas and a nicely served breakfast, try Couleurs Café (33-35, rue de la République). You can also pick up a great brioche at an old world bakery (which uses butter only and organic eggs) right in the center of town, called Montero (3, place Ferdinand Buisson). And, if you are looking for a quiet waterside oasis, at the far end of L'île aux Brocantes (the antiques village across from the flea market), you'll find café Chez Nane, surrounded by lush vegetation and shaded by a tall ficus tree.

For a special meal, head out of town about six kilometers to the Mas de Cure Bourse (120, chemin de la Serre, route de Caumont, tel. 04-90-38-16-58), a tastefully-restored inn and restaurant, surrounded by high hedges and tall trees. The inn has two dining areas, one with wooden beams, a large stone fireplace (so welcome in winter) and a wall filled with brilliantly colorful *barbotine* plates. The restaurant serves inventive, but locally grounded, cuisine. It's not inexpensive, but the food is great, the service excellent and the surroundings very appealing. After dinner, driving along the little roads back into town, you might—as we did—run into a few hares, crisscrossing your path.

OTHER NEARBY MARKETS

For a very down-home market, at the other end of the spectrum from L'Isle-sur-la-Sorgue, there is Montfavet, in the Quartier Bompas, route de Marseille, on Saturday mornings (see Avignon above).

THE

Flea Markets

of

SOUTHWEST FRANCE

THE
Flea Markets
of
SOUTHWEST FRANCE

✦

ABOUT THE REGION

A REGION RECENTLY REDISCOVERED BY VISITORS TO FRANCE, THE SOUTHWEST IS BOTH STUNNING IN ITS NATURAL BEAUTY AND FORWARD-LOOKING IN ITS character. There is a real irony here. While a perhaps less commanding tourism destination than other spots, in terms of the economic and intellectual life of France this is a vigorous and exciting place.

There is a tremendous variety in the geography of this region. The flat, gentle Mediterranean coastline is quite different from the cliff-edged shores of the more turbulent Atlantic in the Pays Basque, and different again from the sand dunes and pine forests along the coast further north, toward Bordeaux. Inland, the lush green fields and dark stone towns of the Dordogne are in stark contrast to the dry, blasted-looking landscape to the southeast, near Montpellier. But, despite the wide diversity in the landscape, there is a unifying feature in this region—a feeling of space and openness and an easy coexistence between nature and the manmade world.

There is also a big contrast in the architecture in this region. Montpellier and Nîmes, for example, closely resemble Provençal towns, in their light stone buildings and open squares. As you approach Toulouse a transformation occurs, with imposing brick buildings in rose tones. Bordeaux is a gracious and elegant city, while the Pays Basque has a look all of its own, with its white buildings, red tiled roofs and red and green shutters.

But architectural differences aside, there are common features here as well—the urban centers are energized by large university populations, a vigorous intelletual life and innovations in the scientific and technological spheres. Huge revitalization projects have also been undertaken in recent years. The center of Bordeaux, for example, with its whisper-quiet tramway system, pedestrian streets and well-scrubbed and lit buildings and squares, offers an impressive example of urban planning at its best.

ABOUT THE MARKETS

There are a surprising number of flea markets in the southwest—considering the largely rural nature of this region—particularly in the east around Montpellier and in the bottom corner, in the Pays Basque. These are generally down-to-earth, no-frills markets, rather than upscale, high-end affairs (with the very notable exception of the monthly market in Toulouse). These markets would especially appeal to bargain hunters willing and keen to forage around to find something they want. Some of the markets will have less interest for general tourists, although for those who do not expect the French way of life to always be presented in a pristine manner, these are fun markets to explore.

As for the kinds of things you will find here, not surprisingly there is a focus on functional collectibles connected to daily, rural life—rustic tools and implements, kitchenware, linens, ceramics, solid wooden furniture and garden accessories. There are a number of regional items to look out for—the dishware, in simple white with navy and burgundy lines, from the Pays Basque, the rustic glazed ceramics and pots from the area around Montpellier, the wonderful high-quality woven linens, often with navy and red stripes, from Béarn and the Pays Basque, the more colorful bright linens from the Catalan region around Perpignan, wine collectibles (this is, after all, a renowned winemaking region), objects (from tiles to jewelry) decorated with the Basque cross, "cowboy" gear from the Camargue, religious souvenirs from Lourdes, chocolate molds (Bayonne, in the Pays Basque, has long been a chocolate-making center) and sports collectibles (related to hugely popular rugby and the Basque game of *pelota*).

WHEN TO GO ✣ HOW TO TRAVEL

While this is a generally mild part of France (Biarritz, for example, not infrequently records the highest daytime temperatures in the winter), the winter months can be unpredictable. July and August, on the other hand, can be oppressively hot. Your best bet is to try to come here in the spring or fall, when the weather is more reasonable and the touristy parts of the region (particularly the Pays Basque and the Dordogne) are not too crowded.

If you only plan to visit the bigger towns and cities, the train is perhaps the best way to travel. Train service is good throughout most of the region, even extending into the smaller centers of the Pays Basque. However, if you want to see flea markets that are more off the beaten track, I would advise renting a car, which will also allow you to explore the wonderful coastline and lush interior. Be warned, though, that the autoroutes in this area—particularly between Montpellier and Bordeaux—are busy and stressful, with a huge number of trucks.

AHETZE
Third Sunday of the month

Number of Vendors: 200 · Price-Quality: ⚜⚜
Scenic Value: ⚜⚜–⚜⚜⚜ · Amenities Nearby: ⚜⚜

FEATURED ITEMS

kitchenware, Basque linens, Basque dishes, tools, farm implements, hardware, furniture, secondhand clothing, toys, rustic items generally

MARKET DETAILS

The small village of Ahetze, about eight kilometers to the east of Saint-Jean-de-Luz, has a large flea market on the third Sunday of the month, all day, in the center of town. This is a market you will need a car to access. Follow signs to Ahetze and park along the side of the road as you enter the town, as finding a spot in the center can be difficult.

SAINT-JEAN-DE-LUZ, THE CLOSEST TOWN TO THE AHETZE FLEA MARKET, IS, I MUST CONFESS, MY FAVORITE TOWN IN FRANCE. LOCATED RIGHT ON THE Atlantic coast in the wonderful Pays Basque, just north of the Spanish border, the setting could not be more spectacular. The town faces a wide expanse of sandy beach, in a bay protected from the waves of the Atlantic, with lush green slopes

behind. As is typical of this region, the architecture has that pleasing uniformity of whitewashed buildings, with wooden shutters and windows painted in either red or green (the Basque colors) and with rust-colored tiled roofs. The style is the perfect accompaniment to the crisp and clear juxtaposition of mountains and sea. And nothing is more exhilarating than a brisk walk along the town's coastal path in the sunshine, looking back at the Basque buildings lining the water.

The town itself, though inundated with tourists during the summer, somehow still manages to retain some of its character as a fishing port, with charming red and green boats bobbing in its harbor. Fishing has been the mainstay of this place for centuries, although the whales and cod have given way to tuna, sardines and anchovies. The most memorable historical event in the town was the marriage in 1660 of Louis the XIV to Maria Teresa, daughter of the King of Spain, in the town's oak-galleried Saint Jean-Baptiste church. Today, the French-Spanish merger is still evident in the mix of visitors to this place. Not only will you hear a lot of Spanish on the pedestrian streets of the town, but also Basque—the language of this trans-border region, whose origins remain a mystery.

Apart from Saint-Jean-de-Luz—and its much more chic (and less typically Basque) neighbor to the north, Biarritz—there are a number of communities well worth a visit, to absorb the unique flavor of this corner of France: Bayonne, the region's cultural capital, and the charming villages of Ascain, Ainhoa, Espelette and Saint-Jean-Pied-du-Port, to name a few.

There is also the tiny village of Ahetze, about a 15-minute drive from Saint-Jean-de-Luz, over rolling, green pastures dotted with cattle. The population here is small —perhaps less than a thousand—but the community has its whitewashed Basque church, a charming bar and restaurant, a community center and a *fronton*, the tall wall (with a Basque cross) against which the Basque sport *pelota* is played.

THE MARKET

The largest flea market in the Pays Basque takes place in Ahetze, on the third Sunday of the month all day. This is a busy event, with cars lining the sides of the road leading in and out of town. Many have Spanish license plates; after all, the border is only about 25 kilometers away. The atmosphere is pleasant and convivial. You certainly get the impression that this is a popular monthly event in the community, offering an opportunity for socializing as well as browsing.

About 200 vendors set up their wares throughout the town, in a parking lot, a small park and around the community center, by the *fronton*. Some of the vendors have their goods nicely displayed on tables arranged in rows under umbrellas, while others simply put them out on blankets on the ground. Many of those selling in this market appear to be *particuliers*, regular people from around the region. Several are here to sell their secondhand belongings—clothes, toys, bits and pieces of kitchenware, linens, tools, etc. Others offer collectibles typical of this region—the wonderful and beautifully woven Basque linens, in white with dark red and navy stripes (and more recently red and green), and Basque dishes, in white with dark red and navy lines. There are also lots of wooden items for sale, including small carved boxes and solid pieces of furniture. Some of the collectibles—old tiles and jewelry, for example —sport the signature Basque cross.

OTHER THINGS TO DO

The village of Ahetze has a cozy bar/restaurant right by the flea market, called

Hiriartia, decorated with rugby memorabilia. But if you want to check out some of the other little towns in the region, try Espelette, which has a charming vine-covered hotel decorated with long strands of peppers (a local specialty), called Hotel Euzkadi (285, rue Karrika Nagusia, tel. 05-59-93-91-88). The restaurant is appealing, with beamed ceilings and large armoires filled with Basque linens, and the food is hearty and good.

Saint-Jean-de-Luz itself has several interesting restaurants. I particularly like a little place on the restaurant-lined rue de la République, called Pasaka (11, rue de la République, tel. 05-59-26-05-17) where I had the Basque dish *axoa* (a flavorful stew based on ground veal), *gateau Basque*, a plain buttery flat cake and *brebis* (the Basque sheep's milk cheese), served with a dark cherry sauce. For another specialty, *ttoro* (a local version of bouillabaisse), I recommend Petit Grill Basque (Chez Maya) (2, rue Saint-Jacques, tel. 05-59-26-80-76). This small appealing place, with Basque dishware and linens, is also jammed with regional collectibles. The ceiling has an old wooden fan draped with cloth that can be operated from the kitchen by pulling periodically on a rope (as the owner delighted in showing us).

Saint-Jean-de-Luz is also noted for its several stores selling Basque linens, from the more traditional finely woven ones in classic Basque designs and shades to the modern, brilliantly colorful linens at stores like Jean Vier. As you are walking around, try the fresh caramels at Pariès, and the *macarons* at Maison Adam, both on the rue Gambetta. (A café next to the beach in Biarritz—Café Dodin—also serves delicious caramels.) If you get to the larger, classically Basque town of Bayonne, just north of Biarritz, there are two celebrated places for chocolates on the rue Port Neuf—Cazenave and Daranatz. Bayonne is also home to the celebrated Musée Basque (37, quai des Corsaires, tel. 05-59-59-08-98).

OTHER NEARBY MARKETS

Several other flea markets are regularly held in this region. Anglet, a small community adjacent to Biarritz, has a large flea market on the fourth Saturday of the month, but check regarding the schedule in the case of months with five Saturdays (when it may take place on the fifth one). The market takes place all day in the Esplanade de Quintaou. Anglet also has a small all-day *brocante* market on the second Sunday of the month in the place des Cinq Cantons. Ciboure, the community just across the harbor from Saint-Jean-de-Luz, has a moderate-sized market on the first Sunday of the month, all day, in the Quartier Untxin. The small village of Ascain, just a few kilometers southwest of Saint-Jean-de-Luz, hosts a small market on the second Saturday of the month, all day, in the center of town, in front of the *fronton*. Finally, Bayonne has a small flea market on Friday mornings, at the Carreau des Halles.

BORDEAUX
Sunday morning

Number of Vendors: 80 to 100 · Price-Quality: ❦ ❦
Scenic Value: ❦ ❦ · Amenities Nearby: ❦ ❦ – ⚜ ⚜ ⚜

FEATURED ITEMS

kitchenware, tools, rustic items, books, paintings, glassware,
porcelain and ceramics, furniture

MARKET DETAILS

Bordeaux's good-sized flea market takes place on Sunday mornings in the southeastern end of town, in the place Canteloup (popularly referred to as the place Saint-Michel) in front of the Saint-Michel church. If arriving by car, the market is just west of the Garonne River, not far from the Pont de Pierre. There is some parking available along the streets which lead into the place Canteloup. If arriving by train, the market is about a 20-minute walk from the station. As you exit, follow the cours de la Marne, turn right on the rue Leyteire and right again on the rue des Cordeliers, which goes into the place Canteloup.

BORDEAUX IS ONE OF SEVERAL CITIES IN FRANCE WHICH HAS ENJOYED A REAL RENAISSANCE IN RECENT YEARS. ITS ALREADY IMPRESSIVE EIGHTEENTH-century center, with its ornate stone edifices and splendid squares, has benefited from an extensive facelift. Buildings which had become coated in black have been scrubbed clean, cars have been diverted from city streets, and quiet and efficient trams now run through the center, whisking people in from the periphery. A number of streets are devoted to pedestrians and cyclists, and public buildings and squares have been given new life with dramatic lighting. The result is impressive indeed. Now offering a great space for residents and tourists alike, Bordeaux is a model for other similarly-sized European cities of what can be achieved by a clever blend of old and new.

Of course, the city's officials had much to inspire them. Bordeaux is blessed with some truly splendid spots—the place Gambetta (with its English garden), site of many beheadings during the French Revolution; the wide, high-end shopping street, the cours de l'Intendance; the graceful place de la Comédie (with its ornate Grand Théâtre); the intimate place du Parlement; and the Cathédrale Saint-André, and its square, to name a few.

There is a noticeably modern, forward-looking tone to this town. Perhaps it has something to do with the city's cosmopolitan past and its historical links with the outside world, especially Britain. After all, the city was under English control for three centuries during the Middle Ages, when it prospered in trading wine, much of it exported to England. The wine business still plays an important role in the city's economic life today.

THE MARKET

Bordeaux's Sunday morning flea market (there are also several vendors here on Thursday mornings) is a substantial one. From 80 to 100 sellers (depending on the season and the weather) set up around the basilique Saint-Michel in the southeast end of town, an area that has yet to succumb to the renovators' touch. The narrow streets which lead into the square, though un-restored, do have their charms.

Like its environs, this is an unpolished, down-home flea market, where most of the vendors simply set out their wares on the ground, in crates or piled on blankets. There is, however, a fair range in the things you can find here. While several vendors sell odds-and-ends dishware, glassware, kitchen utensils and tools (even some secondhand clothes), others concentrate on more decorative collectibles—Art Deco figurines, lamps, armoires, paintings and porcelain. Some items typical of the region can be found scattered about—for example, ceramics from the Pays Basque and linens from both Béarn and the Pays Basque.

This is a friendly market, where vendors stand about chatting with each other and with the market's wide-ranging clientele—dealers, bourgeois Bordelais, men and women in traditional Middle Eastern garb and tourists. And some good finds can be made—particularly early in the morning—as real collectibles are sometimes intermixed with everyday kitchen crockery. Vendors are also willing to bargain, making this a promising market for those looking for a good find at a good price, who don't mind expending a bit of energy in the process. On the other hand, if your time is limited, and you prefer your collectibles to come to you in more refined circumstances, this is probably not the place for you.

OTHER THINGS TO DO

After checking out the market, you might want to stop in for a drink in the café across the square, in the Passage Saint-Michel, which houses the stalls of several antiques dealers. There is also a small food market just south of here, the Marché des Capucins, where I stumbled upon some of the best bread I have found in France. Otherwise, you will likely want to return to the more pristine center of town.

One of the most congenial spots is the place du Parlement, where kids play freely, even at night, around its beautiful fountain. In the square is a spacious and pleasant café/restaurant that serves a good breakfast (somewhat of a rarity in France) and lunch, called Karl (6, place du Parlement, tel. 05-56-81-01-00); it also has wireless internet. Le Bistrot d'Edouard (16, place du Parlement, tel. 05-56-81-48-87) across the way, offers a better spot for people-gazing than for eating perhaps, but is certainly adequate.

For a Bordelais dessert specialty as you are wandering around, try *canelés* (small spongy, caramelized cakes) at one of the very smart Baillardran shops you will see around town (for example, along the cours de l'Intendance, at number 55). This very tasty treat, of apparently religious origin, dates back to the sixteenth century.

If you have a car, I highly recommend a visit to Arcachon, on the coast just over an hour's drive west from Bordeaux. Not only are the sandy beaches here stupendous, but the *ville d'hiver*—with its winding streets and whimsical brick mansions—is truly magical. Have lunch at nautical-looking Chez Yvette (59, boulevard de Général Leclerc, tel. 05-56-83-05-11), a local institution known for its oysters (an Arcachon specialty) and other seafood. And then, if you have time, head to the giant Dune du Pyla; your 15-minute ascent will be amply rewarded by a panoramic view of the coastline and the pine forests behind.

OTHER NEARBY MARKETS

This corner of France is not blessed with many significant flea markets. However, there is a modest-sized one on the second Saturday of the month, all day, in Libourne, to the northeast of Bordeaux, in the place Abel sur Champ. A similarly-sized market takes place on the first Sunday of the month, all day, in Fronsac, right next to Libourne, at the Espace Plaisance.

LUNEL
Saturday morning

Number of Vendors: 120 to 150 · Price‑Quality: ✤ – ✤ ✤
Scenic Value: ✤ · Amenities Nearby: ✤ – ✤ ✤

FEATURED ITEMS

kitchenware, tools, Provençal quilts (boutis), riding gear, boules, tins, baskets, garden accessories, rustic items generally

MARKET DETAILS

The Lunel flea market takes place on Saturday mornings, starting early. If arriving by car, head for the center of town. You will have no trouble finding the market, which is held by the place des Arènes. Parking is available in the lot next to the market.

THE CAMARGUE, THE CORNER OF FRANCE SOUTHWEST AND SOUTHEAST OF ARLES, IS A STRANGE AND FLAT REGION, INHABITED BY BLACK BULLS, WHITE horses and, at one time, *gardiens*—the French equivalent to cowboys—who tended them. Today, little remains of the *gardiens*, but you will still see bulls and horses as you meander through this bucolic region which stretches out into the delta of the Rhône River. This is an area with few tourist towns, apart from Les

Saintes-Maries-de-la-Mer, right on the coast, and the thirteenth-century walled town of Aigues-Mortes, which has the eerie feel of a place fixed in time.

Lunel, about 20 kilometers to the north of Aigues-Mortes, on the western edge of this region, feels a bit like a Wild West frontier town *à la française*. Just a few kilometers outside of Lunel in most directions, you are back in the vast countryside, dotted with low-lying farms. The town itself has that dusty feel of a not very prosperous place that time has passed by, as it seems indeed to have done. But while perhaps of little touristic interest, Lunel is a real, workaday town, which also has a busy weekly flea market.

THE MARKET

Lunel's market, held on Saturday mornings, is fairly substantial, with up to 150 vendors. Like the town itself, it is a very no-nonsense, no-frills affair, where ordinary people rather than dealers (for the most part) offer their wares to the largely local clientele. While many seem to be selling their own used belongings—clothing, toys, and bits and pieces of kitchenware, for example—some concentrate more on collectibles, albeit mostly of the rustic, as opposed to decorative, sort.

This is a market where you will likely see collectibles from the Camargue and nearby areas—tools, riding gear and boots, traditional Provençal clothing, and the printed Provençal quilts known as *boutis*. You will also find agricultural implements, garden pots and accessories, hardware and *boules*. Bargaining is expected, not discouraged, though prices are generally low to begin with.

This is emphatically not a market for general tourists, or for collectors looking for fine collectibles. It is also not a place for those who do not relish wading through a fair amount of junk to unearth a treasure. On the other hand, if the thrill of the chase is what motivates you, this is one of those markets where such efforts can be rewarded, especially if you come early. Not only might you find something interesting, it will likely be a bargain. The last time I was here I bought a finely woven old tablecloth from the Pays Basque for two euros, and was very tempted by a pair of old metal *boules* selling for five. I would not go out of my way to check out this market, but if you are in the area on a Saturday, a quick stopover here may prove fruitful.

OTHER THINGS TO DO

After visiting the market, you will not be tempted to linger long in Lunel. For those interested in getting a better idea of the way of life in the Camargue and its traditions, I recommend a visit to the Musée Camarguais (Mas du Pont de Rousty, tel. 04-90-97-10-82), off the D570 to the southwest of Arles, as well as a glimpse at nearby Les Saintes-Maries-de-la-Mer and Aigues-Mortes.

OTHER NEARBY MARKETS

Another flea market takes place on Saturday morning (from mid-October to mid-June) in nearby Palavas-les-Flots, on the coast a few kilometers to the west. This market is also of the down-home variety, with a few collectibles mixed in with a lot of very uninteresting secondhand goods. But, as in the case of Lunel, your efforts in rummaging through this market may sometimes be rewarded.

MONTPELLIER
Sunday morning

Number of Vendors: 200 · Price-Quality: ❧ – ❧ ❧
Scenic Value: ❧ · Amenities Nearby: ❧ – ❧ ❧

FEATURED ITEMS

prints, paintings, tins, coffee mills, café au lait bowls, tools, linens, toys, ceramics, travel trunks, some furniture, enamelware, rustic ware generally

MARKET DETAILS

Montpellier's giant flea market takes place every Sunday morning at l'Espace Mosson (1, rond-point Schumann, La Paillade), just northwest of the center of town. If arriving by car from the autoroute, take exit 31 and follow signs to Mosson. You will come across a lot of cars parked along the side of the road. Do the same and follow the crowds heading to the market site itself.

AT FIRST BLUSH, MONTPELLIER MAY SEEM A BIT OF A DISAPPOINTMENT, AS YOU EXIT THE AUTOROUTE AMID FAST FOOD JOINTS AND LARGE BOX STORES. AND driving into the center can be a challenge, with roads going off in every direction and the signage less than useful; it almost seems like some perverse person was determined to make the route as circuitous as possible. But once finally installed in a massive underground parking lot (fairly unavoidable) and upon emerging into the enormous place de la Comédie, you quickly see the charms of this place. The giant central square, called l'Oeuf by the locals because of its elongated shape, is ringed with busy cafés, where people-watching and sunbathing seem to be the primary concerns. Sitting here is fun; this is a young and vibrant place, with an average age of about 25.

For more than five centuries, Montpellier has been known as a university town; its medical faculty is particularly renowned in France. The town's prominence, however, goes back much further. A thousand years ago, it was already a main trading center and, despite periods of turbulence, for example, during the seventeenth-century persecution of Protestants in the Wars of Religion, it has maintained its stature.

Montpellier has an especially appealing old center which radiates from the place de la Comédie. The maze of narrow, well-polished pedestrian streets is filled with shoppers and strollers on a sunny Saturday afternoon. A sense of well-being pervades, helped no doubt by the energy and youthfulness of the crowds.

THE MARKET

Montpellier's Sunday flea market (which takes place a few kilometers west of the center of town) is very large and sprawling, with upwards of 200 vendors on an average day. The setting—a large parking lot called l'Espace Mosson, surrounded by unappealing apartment blocks—is less than charming. When you first arrive, you are struck by the number of stalls selling cheap new goods. You are also struck by the crowds. This market is very popular among nearby residents, trendy young people looking for a vintage find and dealers scavenging for bargains.

Once you start to wend your way through the rows of stalls here, you will begin to appreciate the buying opportunities this market has to offer, as well as its charms. After rows of Middle Eastern cooking gear and spices, and lots of second-hand junk, you start to see vendors selling actual collectibles—albeit not high-end ones. Here you will find old kitchenware, enamel ware, old tins and rustic items of all kinds—neither cleaned nor polished—and not very nicely presented.

Then, as you reach the far corner, under a long row of pines, you will spot the higher quality collectibles (comparable to those found in the *brocante* markets of Provence and even the Côte d'Azur). Here, the things for sale—linens, paintings, statues, garden pots, regional ceramics, Provençal quilts—are well-scrubbed and shined, and attractively displayed. Of course, prices follow accordingly, although prices here are quite reasonable compared to other markets.

The atmosphere at this market is laid-back and festive, particularly on a warm, sunny day. In the middle are several food trucks, with tables and chairs set out, offering all kinds of snacks—*merguez* (spicy sausages), *andouillettes* (tripe sausages), *frites*, *brochettes de magret de canard* (skewered ducks' breast) and kebabs. And, after a bit of lunch, you can pick up a bunch of fresh mint or coriander on your way out.

While I really like this market, and would recommend it to people with different collecting tastes, this is one aimed at those who do not mind crowds and a down-to-earth, unpolished scene.

OTHER THINGS TO DO

A reasonably-priced restaurant in Montpellier, popular with the locals and tucked away in the pedestrian streets of the old town, is Le Bouchon Saint-Roch, in the place

Saint-Roch (15, rue du plan d'Agde, tel. 04-67-60-94-18). A very pleasant spot for a beer or a light lunch on the *terrasse* is Toast Tea (7, rue de Vallat, tel. 04-67-60-87-87), also in the pedestrian streets behind l'Oeuf.

OTHER NEARBY MARKETS

Apart from Lunel's Saturday morning and Sète's Sunday morning markets (featured above and below)—both within a 30- to 40-minute drive from Montpellier—the small town of Palavas-les-Flots, on the coast just south of Montpellier, has a sprawling, no-nonsense flea market on Saturday mornings, from mid-October to mid-June.

SETE
Sunday morning

Number of Vendors: 120 to 150 (more in summer) · Price-Quality: ⚜–⚜⚜
Scenic Value: ⚜–⚜⚜ · Amenities Nearby: ⚜–⚜⚜

FEATURED ITEMS

kitchenware, secondhand clothing, toys, linens, tools,
books, rustic items generally

MARKET DETAILS

Sète's flea market takes place on Sunday mornings in the place de la République in the northwest part of town. If arriving by car, follow signs to the center, crossing to the west of the Canal de Sète which runs north from the sea. If you cross at the Pont de la Civette, follow the rue Général de Gaulle west (it becomes the avenue Marx Dormoy). At the end, by the Jardin du Château d'Eau, jog to the right (north) and then west on the rue du Maire Aussenac. Turn right (north) on the rue de la Révolution, which leads into the place de la République, the site of the market. Parking is available on the street near the square. If arriving by train, the market is within easy walking distance southwest of the station. Cross the canal to the west, at the Pont Sadi Carnot, turn south (left) on the quai de Bosc, right at the rue du 4 Septembre,

and then, west of the rue Rouget de Lisle, follow the rue Daniel west to the place de la République.

Sète is a real, workaday town, like many of the communities in the region around Montpellier. It is located in an appealing setting, on a mound of land above the sea, and surrounded by flat coastline. This is a busy fishing town and port, as the many boats tied up along its canal attest. But, unlike other fishing towns, where tourism seems to have long overtaken fishing as the primary activity, this place is the real thing, as you quickly realize as you roam through its unassuming streets.

Though not a big tourist draw, Sète is a pleasant place (first impressions as you head in from the autoroute notwithstanding). A row of pastel buildings lines the canal on one side, accented by brightly colored boats in all shapes and sizes. And on the west side of the canal, several restaurants offer fish and seafood of all kinds, to diners seated outside.

THE MARKET

The Sète market, like the town itself, is an unpretentious, no-frills affair. People come here to sell their secondhand belongings—clothes, toys and books, as well as old kitchenware. Much of it is of little interest to collectors, with those rare but exciting exceptions. For that reason, this is one of those markets where it is best to arrive early if you hope to make a good find. Prices are quite low and if you do find something interesting, you will likely not have to pay much for it.

The market takes place on Sunday mornings in the place de la République in the northwest corner of town. The setting is not especially attractive—the square is surrounded by lots of fairly old, not particularly nice buildings. But this is a good-sized market, at least in the summer when there may be as many as 300 vendors (with less than half that in the winter). Most of the collectibles to be found here are of the rustic, everyday sort—enamelware, copper pots, coffee mills, garden pots, ceramics, metal bottle carriers, old baskets. This is not a market for those interested in finer, more decorative pieces, although you will see a fair number of books and some higher quality dishware. Vendors are particularly friendly—happy to engage in conversation and willing to bargain.

OTHER THINGS TO DO

If you are finished with the market around lunch-time, check out one of the canal-side restaurants. A three-course prix fixe lunch can be had here for around 15 euros.

OTHER NEARBY MARKETS

For more of a collectibles market, head to nearby Marseillan-Plage, just a few kilometers west along the coast on the N112. This market takes place near the tourist office, all day, on both Saturday and Sunday.

ALLÉES JULES GUESDE MARKET

First Friday, Saturday and Sunday of the month, except October

Number of Vendors: 140 · Price-Quality: ❀ ❀ ❀ – ❀ ❀ ❀ ❀

Scenic Value: ❀ ❀ – ❀ ❀ ❀ · Amenities Nearby: ❀ ❀ ❀

FEATURED ITEMS

furniture, porcelain, silver, books, militaria, linens, toys, paintings,
50s and 60s, African art, Art Deco, sports collectibles

PLACE SAINT-SERNIN MARKET

Saturday and Sunday morning

Number of Vendors: 50 to 80 (more on Sunday) · Price-Quality: ❀ ❀

Scenic Value: ❀ ❀ ❀ · Amenities Nearby: ❀ ❀ ❀

FEATURED ITEMS

kitchenware, tools, books, agricultural items,
ceramics, rustic items generally

MARKET DETAILS

The Allées Jules Guesde flea market takes place on the first Friday, Saturday and Sunday of the month (except October), all day, in the south end of town, off the Grand Rond. If arriving by car, you should be able to find parking on the street nearby. If arriving by train, it is about a 30-minute walk to the market. From the station, follow the allées Jean Jaurès to the boulevard Lazare Carnot, and take that south (it turns into the allées François Verdier) to the Grand Rond. Veer to the southwest (right) and you will come upon the allées Jules Guesde.

The place Saint-Sernin market takes place on both Saturday and Sunday morning around the basilique Saint-Sernin, in the center of the *vieille ville*. If arriving by car, try to find parking along the boulevard de Strasbourg, a few blocks east of the market. If arriving by train, take the rue de Bayard west to the boulevard de Strasbourg, then the rue Bellegard to the place Saint-Sernin.

TOULOUSE IS A BEAUTIFUL AND LIVELY CITY. IT IS ALSO A BUSTLING ECONOMIC CENTER, ACTIVE IN BOTH THE HIGH-TECH AND AERONAUTICS INDUSTRIES. (Airbus has its headquarters here, and its planes are assembled just west of town.) Due, in part, to the number of foreigners who come to work in these industries, there is a very cosmopolitan feel to this place, but Toulouse's cosmopolitan credentials are well-rooted. Already subject to several external influences—Roman, Gaul, Christian, Visigoth and Frankish—a thousand years ago, Toulouse was the base of the Counts of Toulouse (noted for their patronage of the troubadours) until the thirteenth century.

The *vieille ville* is particularly impressive, with the extraordinary basilique Saint-Sernin (which resembles an elaborate, multi-layered brick cake), the majestic place du Capitole (great for people-watching) and the many winding narrow streets which open onto smaller, pretty squares. And the Garonne River which forms the western edge of the city center adds a nice pastoral touch.

The city's soft red brick buildings have earned it the nickname the *ville rose*, but it is also "rose" in terms of its politics. This area of France is a bastion of the Socialist Party and of left- wing politics generally, and Toulouse is a part of that trend. There is a palpable openness here, which may also have something to do with its large student body. At over 100,000, it represents about a seventh of the city's total population, contributing to its dynamic tone.

ALLÉES JULES GUESDE MARKET

The Allées Jules Guesde flea market is both large and of high quality, making it perhaps the finest in this part of France. It takes place on the first Friday, Saturday and Sunday of the month (except October), all day, along the allées Jules Guesde, which radiates off the Grand Rond in the southern end of town. About 140 vendors set up their wares here under large canopies, on both sides of two long rows in the middle of the wide avenue. The effect is very appealing (as well as offering protection from inclement weather). Each stall is like a mini-theatrical set, with the wares arranged attractively and appealingly.

This is a high-end market, where you will find a very wide variety of fine, well-polished and pristine collectibles. Vendors focus on particular items—good quality linens, paintings, old toys, books, silver, porcelain, furniture, 50s and 60s collectibles, African art, vintage clothing, cameras, militaria, lamps and chandeliers, sports gear and tapestries. (The last time I came, I noticed one vendor with a large quantity of

violin bows, another with canes, and yet another with old keys.) While the emphasis is on decorative pieces, you will also see well-shined tools and rustic wooden items. Some of the wares are very reflective of this region and its history—for example, riding gear, rugby memorabilia and the wicker scoops used for playing *pelota* (a popular sport in the Pays Basque and neighboring areas).

Prices are quite high. These merchants are well aware of the value of their goods. For them, this is serious business and they are quite matter-of-fact about it. I do find the dealers somewhat standoffish, and not particularly keen to engage in conversation, but they become more talkative when you show real interest in their wares. In any event, you are here to buy, and you can be quite confident that, if you do find something here, it will be of good quality. Even if you do not buy anything, you will find this an interesting market, and a fun way to spend a couple of hours.

At lunchtime, it is amusing to watch the vendors sit down in small groups at beautifully set tables, drinking wine and consuming plates of *magret de canard* (duck breast), *cassoulet* (a southwestern casserole of beans, sausages, pork and duck) and other local specialties—no sandwiches for these folks. Some prepare their own meals, cooked on little stoves in their booths, while others purchase them from the food vans at either end of the market. You can follow suit, and sit down for lunch at the tables set out in front—in addition to *magret*, *confit de canard* (duck preserved in its own fat) and steak, you can order some Champagne, at only three-and-a-half euros a glass.

PLACE SAINT-SERNIN MARKET

On Saturday and Sunday morning a much more down-home flea market takes

place around the basilique Saint-Sernin. Sunday is the better day to come as the market is much busier then (with many more vendors). At this moderate-sized market you will find a variety of everyday kitchen collectibles (dishes, pots and pans, utensils, glassware, etc.), tools, ceramic jugs, rustic farming collectibles, paintings and prints, books and some furniture. Prices are modest to moderate. (For, example, the last time I was here I purchased ten ceramic Epiphany *fèves* for one euro—they normally sell for a euro each.)

This is a market for bargain hunters, but it would also appeal to general visitors, as it is set right in the center of the most beautiful part of Toulouse. It also encircles one of the most appealing churches in France, so if not taken with the goods on offer, all you have to do is cast your gaze upward.

OTHER THINGS TO DO

Though I tend to gravitate to less touristy places, I strongly recommend spending some time café-sitting in the elegant place du Capitole. My favorite spot is Le Florida, at number 12; it's casual and the *café au lait* is surprisingly delicious (a real rarity in France). For a really nice meal, try Van Gogh Café on the intimate, out-of-the-way place Saint-Georges (21, tel. 05-61-21-03-15). The food is very fresh and nicely prepared, and the dining room upstairs (if you can't eat outside) is pleasingly decorated in a modern, but not too modern, style. Another good spot, on the place du Président Wilson nearby, is Restaurant Le Bon Vivre (15, place du President Wilson, tel. 05-61-23-07-17), noted for its duck (in all its forms). And, if you'd like to take home a sweet Toulousian specialty, head to Régals (25, rue du Taur, tel. 05-61-21-64-86) for its candied violets.

OTHER NEARBY MARKETS

The little town of Frouzins, just southwest of Toulouse—and north of Muret—has an all day *puces* market on Sunday in the parking lot of the hall Jean Latapie.

INDEX

THE

Flea Markets

About the Author

Sandy Price is an attorney living in Canada. She has lived and traveled extensively in France.

About the Photographer

Originally from Toronto, Emily Laxer spent several years in France during her childhood. She lived with her family in a small village in Provence, where she attended the local one-room school. As a teenager, she returned, this time to Menton in the Côte d'Azur. She attended university (obtaining an undergraduate and master's degree) in Montreal, and most recently began a PhD in sociology at the University of Toronto.